WHAT JESUS
DIDN'T SAY

WHAT JESUS DIDN'T SAY

Gerd Lüdemann

POLEBRIDGE PRESS
Salem, Oregon

Cover and interior design by Robaire Ream

Library of Congress Cataloging-in-Publication Data

Lüdemann, Gerd.

  What Jesus didn't say / Gerd Lüdemann.

    p. cm.

  Includes index.

  ISBN 978-1-59815-030-8 (alk. paper)

  1. Jesus Christ--Words--Extra-canonical parallels. I. Title.

  BS2970.L83 2011

  232.9'54--dc23

                                               2011022734

Dedicated to Tom Hall

for his work on this and previous books of mine

Contents

Introduction

The Problem of the Phenomenon of Fictional Sayings

We cannot do anything against the truth,
but only for the truth.

Paul, 2 Corinthians 13:8

It has long been a truism of Biblical criticism that the New Testament abounds in sayings incorrectly assigned to Jesus or to the context in which they appear. In attempting to reconstruct what Jesus actually said, researchers have largely ignored the invented sayings and concentrated on the authentic passages. In order to assemble as complete a collection of genuine sayings as possible, they have for the most part focused on examining how the genuine sayings are connected and attempting to determine their specific contexts.

In this book I propose to inspect the other side of the coin by considering a selection of the inauthentic words of Jesus—not only those that clearly were invented, but also those that reveal noteworthy alterations to what must have been their original form and intent. In the latter case, of course, it will be necessary to deal with both the genuine and the distorted versions. My collection of inauthentic logia will, I trust, enable the reader to see the fictional sayings as a collective phenomenon worthy of serious consideration. At the same time, the various elements of the genre will yield an important image of the early Christian mentality and thus a better concept of how the early church created itself from its primitive creeds, doctrines, and beliefs.

Three presuppositions underlying my work are the following: first, the authors of the four gospels of the New
Testament are not known even though, for the sake of conve-
nience, I use the conventional designations Matthew, Mark,
Luke, and John; second, the authors were not eyewitnesses;
and third, from the preface to the Gospel of Luke (Luke
1:1–4)[1] we learn important details about how the gospels
were written. Luke provides us with information about the
rise and transmission of the earliest reports about Jesus and
thereby allows us to form a balanced judgment about the
historical value of the Gospels.

> [1]Since many have attempted to compose a narrative about
> the events which have come to fulfillment among us, [2]as
> they have been handed down to us from those who from
> the beginning were themselves eyewitnesses and servants
> of the word, [3]I too have thought it good, since I have
> investigated everything carefully from the start, to write
> them out in order for you, excellent Theophilus, [4]that you
> may know the certain basis of the teaching in which you
> have been instructed. (Luke 1:1–4)

I have imitated the Greek syntax of this magnificently styled
sentence, which is without parallel in the New Testament
and thus testifies to the literary superiority of the author's
work. It is the only passage in the New Testament Gospels in
which an evangelist speaks of his sources, and it provides us
with four important bits of information: *First*, a number of
other authors (he says "many"!) had already written Gospels
(1:1). *Second*, these writers had no more direct knowledge of
the narrated events than Luke did. The only persons who did
have such knowledge were the "eyewitnesses and servants
of the word" whom he thus identifies as the sources of the
tradition (1:2). *Third*, Luke wants to surpass his predecessors
(his use of the verb "attempt" implies a negative assessment

---

1. This preface most likely included Acts (compare Acts 1:1).

of their works), and has therefore investigated everything they have written so as to describe events correctly and in the proper order (1:3). This means he claims to have made many corrections to his predecessors as well as to available oral traditions from the "eyewitnesses and the servants of the word." *Fourth*, according to Luke, his work is intended to serve as a support for faith; that is, his account of events prepares the basis of Christian doctrine (1:4). In other words, faith is grounded in historical realities that cannot be dismissed as delusory.

What emerges from this preface, then, is that at the very beginning stands the oral tradition of the "eyewitnesses and servants of the word" (1:2). None of them has set down his knowledge about Jesus in writing. That happened only later, and apparently more than one or two gospels came into being in this way. But as yet these individual accounts had not come to enjoy widespread or significant respect. Luke has continued this line with his own work.

According to the Two Documents Hypothesis, Luke and Matthew used both Mark and the Sayings Gospel Q,[2] and did so independently of one another, but none of these three sources was composed by eyewitnesses.

I shall include in my analyses selections from the Gospels of Matthew and John, as well as the Gospel of Thomas. This latter text was among those discovered near Nag Hammadi in Upper Egypt in December 1945, and is beyond question of vital importance, since it reflects a tradition that is in some measure independent of those that informed the New Testament.

Before beginning the analysis of the traditions, let me indicate the *criteria* employed for judging the inauthenticity

---

2. "Q" stands for the German "Quelle", meaning "source." It begins with John's preaching of repentance (Luke 3:7b–9) and ends with the promise to Jesus' followers that they will judge the 12 tribes of Israel (Matt 19:28 / Luke 22:28–30).

of purported sayings of Jesus—criteria that arose from my close analysis of all relevant texts incident to writing *Jesus After 2000 Years: What He Really Said and Did* (Amherst, N.Y.: Prometheus Books, 2001).[3] Let me explain that the development of these methodological instruments was not a matter of choosing from a list of established protocols but rather emerged gradually and naturally from an intense, critical examination of a textual corpus. In short, these judgmental guideposts are not deductive in origin, but represent a rigorously inductive process of evaluation.

Criteria of Inauthenticity

First, words are inauthentic in which the risen Lord speaks or is presupposed as the one who speaks, for after his death Jesus no longer spoke.

Second, all reported sayings of Jesus are to be suspected of inauthenticity if they involve situations in a post-Easter community.

Third, like the previous category, serious suspicion attaches to any attribution that reflects the editorial influence of the final author.

Fourth, those words are inauthentic which presuppose a pagan rather than a Jewish audience, for it is certain that Jesus was active in an exclusively Jewish sphere.

Criteria of Authenticity

In our search for inauthentic sayings of Jesus, we must always reckon with the possibility of encountering authentic words. Indeed, they help us to identify the spurious sayings. Therefore, criteria of authenticity have to be established. The most important of them are as follows:

---

3. In the present book I have literally adopted the exegeses of John 10:11–16; 12:44–50; 15:18–16:15; 16:16–33; 17:1–26 by my former assistant Frank Schleritt that appeared in *Jesus After 2000 Years* and benefited from his overall exposition of the Fourth Gospel.

First, the criterion of *offensiveness* must be listed. Examples of offensive sayings of Jesus are the so-called "immoral heroes" who appear in his parables with striking frequency: the person who finds a treasure in the field and buys the field without mentioning the discovery (Matt 13:44) or the unjust steward who, when called to account by his lord, deceives him in order to curry favor with his lord's debtors (Luke 16:1b–7).

Second, the criterion of *difference* is a plausible way of discovering authentic Jesus material. If a reported saying that cannot be derived from the post-Easter communities points to a clash between the communities and Jesus, then one may assume the latter to have spoken the words in question. One example is Jesus' rejection of fasting, a position that differs from the early church's practice of fasting (Mark 2:18–22).

Third, the criterion of *growth* offers a good opportunity to identify authentic Jesus material. The final form of a text can be compared with the inner portion of an onion from which one layer after another has to be peeled. The older— and thus more authentic—a unit of a text, the more it attracts accretions of later tradition. In the ethical tradition of the Sermon on the Mount, for example, Jesus' absolute prohibition of swearing oaths (Matt 5:34a) has been supplemented with several instructions by "Jesus" (Matt 5:34b–37) that in effect annul this proscription.

Fourth, the criterion of *coherence* often highlights authentic sayings of Jesus by showing that a particular statement is in total harmony with assured Jesus material.

Last but not least, it must be noted that the acceptance of a saying's historicity is not identical with that of verbatim authenticity, while a clear lack of historicity will correctly identify something that Jesus cannot have said.

The origins of these reported false sayings range from evangelists to prophets to personally chosen disciples of Jesus, though in no case are we able to identify the actual source. Yet in one case, namely the book of Revelation from the end of the first century, we can demonstrate that some Christians considered Jesus' voice to have persisted a long time after his death. Indeed, some of the sayings in Revelation may have provided source material for Jesus' inauthentic words in the New Testament gospels (see below, pp. 121–29). That, however, is not at issue here; what matters is that a preponderance of the reported sayings of Jesus found in the four canonical gospels are counterfeits that are subject to objective analysis. A representative sampling will be reproduced here to enable a quick overview. In longer texts I have employed capital letters, italics, capitals, and bold-faced type to foster an appreciation of the literary nature of the texts. Along with these, I have used indents to designate poetic texts and/or traditions. I have sought throughout to produce a translation that is both precise as necessary and free as possible. Gender-inclusive language has been employed except when it would prove deceptive by concealing the cultural presuppositions of the authors.

The sayings will be grouped according to chronological-geographical and doctrinal perspectives. The collection of sayings based on the supposed biography of Jesus, entitled "Way Stations in the Life of Jesus," shows that the inauthentic words of Jesus are embedded in a dramatic but fictional history of salvation. The collection of sayings intended to represent the preaching of Jesus, entitled "Topics of Jesus' Preaching," is intended to demonstrate the diversity of the application of invented sayings of Jesus. Where necessary I have included the words of other persons. In order to place Jesus' sayings in a meaningful context, I have sometimes been obliged to include narrative elements that the gospel writers created to set the scene for the words they attribute to Jesus.

The sheer abundance of inauthentic Jesus-sayings shows beyond cavil that very soon after his sudden and dramatic death he became the center of a new faith. It also demonstrates that, from the very beginning, Christians strove to imagine what answers Jesus would offer to the many questions that arose among them. Therefore, when his recalled words seemed no longer appropriate or when no *bona fide* answers were available, utterances had to be revised or invented to suit the existing situation. Behind the inauthentic words of Jesus we can envision a movement the members of which, in order to justify themselves in the face of both internal and external opposition, felt obliged to carry the message of their Lord to the world at large. More than that, however, each invented text bespeaks and communicates a religious certainty that will brook no contradiction. In this, of course, we see reflected the jealous and exclusivist One God of Judaism whose demands of total loyalty and obedience would, in the eyes of antiquity, tolerate no diminution.

Still more important, the pervasiveness of this inauthentic material in the writings of people who represent themselves as purveyors of ultimate truths must both qualify any claims of ethical superiority on behalf of the movement they represent and further suggest the importance of this project for a thoughtful reassessment of their historical pretensions.

INAUTHENTIC SAYINGS OF JESUS IN THE NEW TESTAMENT GOSPELS

Way Stations in the Life of Jesus

1

In the Temple of Jerusalem
The First Words of Jesus

Luke 2:41–52
The twelve-year-old Jesus

[41]And his parents traveled every year to Jerusalem for the feast of the Passover.

[42]When he was twelve years old, they went up (to Jerusalem), according to the custom of the feast. [43]After they had spent all of the days (of the feast) and his parents were returning home, the boy Jesus stayed behind in Jerusalem, but they were unaware of it. [44]Thinking he was in their company, they traveled on for a day. Then they began looking for him among their relatives and friends. [45]When they did not find him, they went back to Jerusalem to look for him. [46]And it happened that after three days they found him in the sanctuary, sitting among the teachers, *listening* **to them** and asking them questions.

[47]But all who *listened* **to him** were amazed at his understanding and answers.

[48]When his parents saw him, they were astonished. His mother said to him, "Child, why have you done this to us? See, **your father** and I have been anxiously *looking for* you."

[49]And he said to them: "Why were you *looking for* me? Did you not know that I must be in what is **my Father's**?"

[50]But they did not understand what he was saying to them.

[51a]And he went down with them and came to Nazareth and was obedient to them.

[51b]And his mother treasured all these things in her heart.

[52]And Jesus increased in wisdom, age, and grace with God and the people.

ARGUMENT AGAINST AUTHENTICITY

Verses 41–45 set the scene. When his family leaves Jerusalem after a pilgrimage, the twelve-year-old Jesus remains behind;

and upon noticing his absence, his parents return to look for him. Verse 46 reports their successful search: Joseph and Mary find Jesus among the teachers in the temple.

Whereas in verse 46 Jesus was the one who listened and asked questions, in verse 47 it is reported that he also gave insightful answers. In verse 48, the subject changes abruptly from the audience to the parents. With Jesus' answer in verse 49—the first words attributed to him in the Gospel of Luke—the point of the story appears in his reply to his mother's question (verse 48). As Son of God, Jesus must be involved in his Father's concerns. In this way Luke distinguishes Jesus' earthly father—who, along with his mother, has searched for Jesus—from his heavenly Father. This higher necessity also determines the details of the history of salvation (see Luke 4:43; 24:7, 26, 44; Acts 1:16; 3:21; 9:16).

In verse 50 the parents react to their child's answer with the incomprehension of human beings reacting to a divine message (Luke 2:33), although verse 51b conflicts with this. The information in verse 51a about the return to Nazareth derives wholly from Luke (2:39). Verse 51b echoes Luke 2:19 and stems from the author (for its inconsistency with verse 50, see above). The maturing of the child described in verse 52 corresponds to Luke 1:80 and 2:40, and to some degree bridges the time gap between this and the baptism and public appearance of the adult Jesus (3:31, 23).

In summary, Luke has taken up a well-rounded individual story and put it into his own words. With the addition of verse 47, he has given as much weight to Jesus' unusual wisdom as to his divine sonship, which is the point of verse 49b.

The original story—that of the wisest child in Israel, who is already knowledgeable in the law—does not presuppose either the miracle of the annunciation (Luke 1:26–38) or that of the virgin birth (2:1–20), nor does it attest knowledge on the part of the parents that their child is the Messiah. The narrative does, of course, contain the theme widespread in antiquity that the extraordinary capacities of a great personality are already apparent in childhood.

We cannot claim a valuable early source for this story, although verse 51b seeks to create such an impression. Like Mark 16:8, it explains why the story became known only relatively late: both the women who discovered the empty tomb and the mother who heard the words of her twelve-year-old were silent for a long time, but the Easter "event" or the fulfilling of the promises led them to speak out at last. Thus, not only is this story is spurious for the reasons just given, but it lacks an historical nucleus.

2

At the Jordan
Words to John the Baptist

Matthew 3:13–15
Fulfill all righteousness

¹³Then Jesus comes from Galilee to the Jordan to John to have himself *baptized* by him.

¹⁴But he sought to prevent him and said, "I need to be *baptized* by you; and you come to me?"

¹⁵But Jesus answered and said to him, "Let it be so now; for it is fitting for us to fulfill all righteousness."

Then he let him.

ARGUMENT AGAINST AUTHENTICITY

The text reworks Mark 1:9–11. Particularly in verse 15 the new interpretation becomes visible. By having himself baptized by John, Jesus "fulfills all righteousness," and thus gives his disciples an example to do likewise. Matthew uses the word "righteousness" seven times (3:15; 5:6, 10, 20; 6:1, 33; 21:32). As a rule it refers to something a human being does. Compare especially Matt 5:20—"If your righteousness does not by far surpass the righteousness of the Scribes and Pharisees, you will not enter the kingdom of God"—and Matt 6:1—"Beware of practicing your righteousness before people in order to be noticed by them; for then you will have no reward from your Father who is in heaven."

Jesus' answer to John at verse 15 constitutes his first utterance in the Gospel of Matthew. It serves as a signal and points forward to Matt 5:17: "Do not think that I have come to abolish the law or the prophets; I have not come to abolish but to fulfill."

This insistence on being baptized by John grows out of early Christian debates. While many Christians regarded

Jesus as sinless (see John 8:46; 2 Cor 5:21; Heb 4:15), they had to explain why Jesus had himself baptized by John, for whom this rite represented the forgiveness of sins (Mark 1:4). Here "Jesus" solves the problem by relating his baptism to a higher purpose.

3

In the Desert
Words to the Devil

Matthew 4:1–11	**Luke 4:1–13**

¹Then Jesus was led by the Spirit into the wilderness, to be **tempted** by the *DEVIL*. ²And after he had fasted forty days and forty nights he became hungry.

[1] ³And the **tempter** came and said to him, "IF YOU ARE THE SON OF GOD, tell these stones to become bread."

⁴But he answered and said, "*It is written*, 'Man will not live by bread alone, but by every word that proceeds from the mouth of God.'" [Deut 8:3]

[2] ⁵Then the *DEVIL* takes him to the holy city and sets him on the pinnacle of the temple ⁶and says to him. "IF YOU ARE THE SON OF GOD, cast yourself down; for *it is written*, 'He will give his ANGELS orders about you; and they will bear you in their hands, so that you do not strike your foot against a stone.'" [Ps 91:11–12]

⁷Jesus said him, "Again *it is written*, 'You shall not **tempt**

¹And Jesus, full of Holy Spirit, returned from the Jordan and was led by the Spirit into the wilderness, ²and was **tempted** forty days by the *DEVIL*. And he ate nothing during those days, and when they were at the end, he became hungry.

[1] ³And the *DEVIL* said to him, "IF YOU ARE THE SON OF GOD, tell this stone to become bread." ⁴And Jesus answered him, "*It is written*: 'Man will not live by bread alone.'" [Deut 8:3]

[3] ⁵And *he led him* up and showed him in an instant all the kingdoms of the world. ⁶And the *DEVIL* said to him, "To you I will give all this power and glory, for it has been delivered to me, and I give it to whom I will. ⁷If you now *WORSHIP* before me, all (that) shall be yours."

⁸Jesus answered and said, "*It is written*
You shall *WORSHIP* as Lord your God
and him only shall you

6

the Lord your God.'" [Deut. 6:16 LXX]

[3] ⁸Last, the DEVIL takes him to a very high mountain and shows him all the kingdoms of the world and their glory and says to him, ⁹"All this I will give you, if you fall down and WORSHIP me."

¹⁰Jesus said to him, "Get away from me, Satan! For *it is written*:

You shall WORSHIP as Lord your God,
and him only shall you serve." [Deut 6:13 LXX]

¹¹Then the DEVIL leaves him, and all at once ANGELS came and ministered to him.

serve." [Deut 6:13 LXX]

[2] ⁹And he *led him* to Jerusalem and set him on the pinnacle of the temple and said to him, "IF YOU ARE THE SON OF GOD, cast yourself down from here; ¹⁰for *it is written*, 'He will give his angels orders about you to preserve you,' ¹¹and 'They will bear you in their hands, so that you do not strike your foot against a stone.'" [Ps 91:11–12]

¹²Jesus answered and said to him, "It is said, 'You shall not **tempt** the Lord your God.'" [Deut 6:16]

¹³And after completing every **temptation**, the DEVIL departed from him until the (appointed) time.

ARGUMENT AGAINST AUTHENTICITY

Writing independently of one another, Matthew and Luke take up Mark's brief account of Jesus' temptation (1:12–13) and expand on it by adapting a text they found in Q (see Matt 4:3–11 and Luke 4:3–12). Matthew seems to preserve the original sequence of the three dialogues between Jesus and the devil given the following observations: (a) "Son of God" occurs in the first two dialogues; (b) the placement of the temptation promising power over the whole world at the end of the exchanges is a climax; and (c) only in the third temptation does the devil reveal that what he really wants is worship, while in the second temptation he hypocritically quotes scripture.

Following Mark's placement of this story, both evangelists locate it at the beginning of the public activity of Jesus.
Together with the proclamation of Jesus' sonship in the previously narrated baptism, this episode forms an effective prelude to the subsequent story of the Son of God. Indeed, the
truth of Jesus' divine sonship is demonstrated both by his
acceptance of baptism and his rejection of the devil.

That the quotations of Scripture partly follow the Greek
translation of the Hebrew Bible (= LXX) is a further reason
to classify these accounts as spurious. Last but not least, no
witness is present, and it is rather unlikely that either Satan or
Jesus would have told the disciples about the event. Be that
as it may, the clearly mythic quality and content of the story
is more than sufficient to make the case for its inauthentic
nature.

4

In the Synagogue of Nazareth
Inaugural Sermon

Luke 4:14–28

*First sermon of Jesus, intended to show him
fulfilling the scriptures and inaugurating
the mission to the gentiles*

[14]And Jesus returned in the power of the Spirit to Galilee. And
news of him resounded through all the surrounding places. [15]And
he taught in their *synagogues* and was praised by all.

[16]And he came to Nazareth, where he had been brought up,
and went according to his custom into the *synagogue* and stood
up to read. [17]And the scroll of the prophet Isaiah was handed to
him, and when he unrolled the scroll, he found the place where it
is written:

> [18]The Spirit of the *LORD* is on me,
> because he has anointed me.
> To preach the good news to the poor
> he has sent me,
> to proclaim *freedom* to the prisoners
> and sight to the blind, [Isa 61:1–2]
> to set at *freedom* those who are oppressed, [Isa 58:6]
> [19]to proclaim a WELCOME year of the *LORD*. [Cf. Lev
> 25:10]

[20]And he rolled up the scroll, gave (it) back to the attendant
and sat down. And all the eyes in the *synagogue* were fixed on
him. [21a]And he began to speak to them, [21b]"Today is this scripture
fulfilled in your hearing."

[22]And all gave testimony about him and marveled at the words
of grace that came from his mouth and said, "Is this not the son
of Joseph?"

[23]And he said to them, "Doubtless you will quote me this
proverb, 'Physician, heal yourself!' And you will say, 'Do also here

in your *fatherland* what we have heard you did in Capernaum.'"
²⁴But he said, "Truly, I say to you, no prophet is WELCOME in his *fatherland*.

²⁵"But in fact, I tell you,
there were many widows in Israel in the days of Elijah, when the heaven was shut for three years and six months and a great famine came over all the land, ²⁶and Elijah was not sent to any of them, except to Zarephath in Sidon, to a woman who was a widow. [Cf. 1 Kings 17:9]

²⁷"And there were many lepers in Israel in the time of the prophet Elisha, and none of them was healed but Naaman the Syrian." [Cf. 2 Kings 5:14]

²⁸All in the *synagogue* were filled with rage when they heard this.

ARGUMENT AGAINST AUTHENTICITY

Here, editing Mark 6, Luke programmatically sets Jesus' inaugural sermon in his hometown of Nazareth. It is the only speech in Luke's Gospel in which Jesus addresses a regular assembly (cf. the corresponding speeches Paul makes in his defense in Acts 22:1–21; 24:10–21; 26:2–23). Further, in Luke's narrative sequence this speech replaces Mark's account of the calling of the first disciples (Mark 1:16–20). Clearly, Luke initiates Jesus' career with this more or less everyday kind of event in order to suggest that the rejection in Nazareth foreshadows his future fate.

Here, Luke apologetically expands Mark: *first* by having Jesus read a prophetic testimony in verses 18–19 and comment on it in verse 21; *second* by the prediction in verses 25–27 that salvation will pass to another people. The latter is a crude distortion of Jesus' view of himself, as it already includes the Gentile mission among his tasks and also contains a strongly anti-Jewish flavor. The former, a quotation from the Greek scriptures, makes a claim of fulfillment, a major theme in Luke (cf. 1:1–4; 24:27, 44). To back it up,

Luke fabricated the saying ascribed to Jesus in verse 21 as an essential element of the story telling. It is unlikely that the pronouncement would have been passed on independently at the oral stage of the transmission of Jesus sayings.

In sum, Jesus' Inauguration Sermon in the Gospel of Luke is fictitious from top to toe.

5

In Galilee

Limiting the Mission of the Disciples to Israel

Matthew 10:5b–15

The charge to the disciples

5b"Do not take the way to the Gentiles
and a TOWN of the Samaritans do not enter!
6*Go* rather to the lost sheep of the house of Israel!

7And when you *go*, preach and say, 'The kingdom of heaven is at hand.'

8Heal the sick,
raise the dead,
cleanse lepers,
drive out demons.
Freely you have received, freely give!

9"Take no gold nor silver nor copper in your belts—10no bag for your journey nor a spare tunic, no shoes and no staff—for a worker is *worthy* of his food.

11"And if you enter a TOWN or a village, find someone who is *worthy* and remain with him until you depart.

12"And if you *go* into a HOUSE, greet it; 13and if the HOUSE is *worthy*, LET YOUR PEACE BLESSING come on it.

"But if it is not *worthy*, LET YOUR PEACE BLESSING return to you.

14"And when people do not receive you and will not hear your words, —depart from that HOUSE or TOWN and shake the dust from your feet!

15"Truly, I say to you, it will be more tolerable for Sodom and Gomorrah on the day of judgment than for this TOWN."

ARGUMENT AGAINST AUTHENTICITY
Matthew has formulated verses 5b–6. Besides, in verses 7–15 he uses Mark 6:8–11 and Q (cf. Luke 10:4–12).

According to Matthew—as demonstrated by verses 5b–6—the preaching of Jesus is addressed both to the disciples and to the people of Israel. The expression "the lost sheep of the house of Israel" has been formulated with a clear allusion to 1 Kgs 22:17, as in Matt 15:24. This parallelism extends also to actions (cf. verses 7–8). For linguistic reasons verse 6 stems from Matthew ("go", "sheep", "lost"), but has a basis in the tradition in that, like Jesus, the disciples originally worked only among Jews.

Matthew consistently sets the disciples in parallel with Jesus (verses 7–8). Like his actions, theirs point to the imminence of the kingdom of God (cf. Matt 4:17). As with him, their preaching is accompanied by mighty acts: raisings of the dead (cf. Matt 9:18–26; 11:5), healings of lepers (cf. Matt 8:2–4; 11:5) and of the possessed (cf. Matt 4:24; 8:16; 8:28–34; 9:32). Matthew has deliberately chosen the actions in verse 8 to emphasize their relationship to the miracles in Matthew 8–9.

The rules about clothing and equipment (verse 9) go back to Q (cf. Q = Luke 10:5–7). Matthew inserts them because for him poverty is of fundamental importance (cf. Matt 6:19–34). For the Q group, it is a matter of demonstrating a shocking poverty and need, which can be related to the beatitude on the poor (Q = Luke 6:20), defenselessness (Q = Luke 6:29), love of enemy (Q = Luke 6:27–28), the break with all earthly kinsfolk (Q = Luke 14:26) and living only for the kingdom of God (Q = Luke 12:31).

In verses 11–15, a unit that depicts mission practice, Matthew combines Mark 6:10–11 with the Q text (cf. Luke 10:8–12).

As for the historical question, the explicit warning against the Gentiles and the Samaritans in verse 5b does not accord with the compassion and ecumenicity of the teacher Jesus who made a Samaritan the exemplar of one of his parables

(Luke 10:19–37). The technical expression "lost sheep of the house of Israel" in verse 6 (cf. Matt 15:24) clearly reflects a Jewish Christian community whose members believed the Christian message to be intended exclusively for Jews.

Note also that Jesus enjoins the disciples to perform the various wonders attributed to him—including even the resurrection of the dead (verse 8). Yet this transfer of power is supposed to have occurred only after Easter, when they engaged in missionary work.

The radically ascetic feature of verses 9–10 cannot be reliably attributed to someone who only a chapter later is characterized as a glutton and a drunkard (Matt 11:19).

The missionary directions in verses 11–14 are rooted in the situation of Easter. The speaker is the "Risen One" (cf. Matt 28:19–20).

The threat in verse 15 derives from the early church (cf. Jude 7).

All in all, the passage is a pastiche of elements chosen to support Matthew's theology and to deal with issues that faced the community for which he was writing.

6

On the Way to Jerusalem
Predictions of Death and Resurrection

Mark 8:31
First prediction of suffering,
death and resurrection

And he began to teach them, "The Son of man must suffer much and be rejected by the elders and the chief priests and the scribes, and be killed, and after three days rise."

Mark 9:31
Second prediction of death
and resurrection

For he was teaching his disciples and said to them, "The Son of man will be handed over to those who will kill him, and, when he is killed, after three days he will rise."

Mark 10:32b–34
Third prediction of death
and resurrection

32bAnd he took the Twelve and began to speak to them about what would happen to him. 33"Look, we are going up to Jerusalem and the Son of man
 will be handed over to the chief priests and scribes.
 And they will *condemn* him to death
 and hand him over to the Gentiles,
34and they will *mock* him and *spit on* him,
 and scourge him,
 and kill him,
 and after three days he will rise."

ARGUMENT AGAINST AUTHENTICITY
The first prediction (8:31) is the starting point for the second and third predictions of the passion and resurrection.

Mark has formulated the two other texts on the basis of this prophecy that had been handed down to him, giving the third prediction special weight by setting its details in close parallel to those of his passion account. Thus, three verbs used in the passion narrative—"condemn" (cf. Mark 14:64), "mock" (cf. Mark 15:20, 31), "spit on" (cf. Mark 14:65; 15:19)—appear in Mark 10:32–34 (on "scourge" cf. Mark 15:15).

By means of these three announcements of the passion, and especially the third, Mark emphasizes that Jesus is going voluntarily to Jerusalem to die; for this is necessary and accords with the will of his Father (cf. Mark 8:31a). Jesus predicts his end, including all the harrowing details, yet he will not alter his determined course.

Perhaps a didactic or homiletic purpose can be discerned: only if Jesus knew in advance of his death and resurrection is he really the Lord of death and life. We see the completion of this development in the Fourth Gospel:

> [17]For this reason the Father loves me, because I lay down my life, that I may take it again. [18]No one takes it away from me, but I lay it down of my own accord. I have the power to lay it down, and I have the power to take it again. This charge I have received from my Father. (John 10:17–18)

As Mark links the third prediction of the passion so closely with the passion narrative, a strong anti-Jewish feature becomes clear (cf. also Matt 21:33–46; 22:1–14; 23:13–28 and John 8:37–45). For with the killing of Jesus the Jewish authorities accomplish the plan they have been cherishing since the beginning of Jesus' public ministry (cf. Mark 3:6: "The Pharisees went out, and immediately held counsel with the Herodians against him, how to destroy him").

As for the historicity of the *threefold* prediction of the passion and resurrection of Jesus, Mark's clearly literary formulation and recognizable intent tell against it. Cf. also the *threefold* denial of Jesus by Peter (Mark 14:66–72).

Arguments against the historicity of the *first* prediction of the passion and resurrection—upon which the second and the third predictions are based—are similar: not only does it place undisguised anti-Judaism in the mouth of a pious Jew, but it is hardly credible that Jesus knew of his resurrection after three days or that his disciples could envision such an event, let alone hope for it, since it would entail his death. At any rate, the prediction of his resurrection was attributed to him at a later stage, and therefore considerable doubt must be attached to the prediction of his own suffering.

7

In Jerusalem
Prediction of the Temple's Destruction

Mark 13:1–2

¹And when he goes out of the temple, one of his disciples says to him, "Teacher, look at these stones and at these buildings!"

²And Jesus said to him, "Do you see these great buildings? Not a stone will be left on another; all will be demolished."

ARGUMENT AGAINST AUTHENTICITY

The astonishment of one of the disciples at the grandeur of the temple in verse 1 serves as the cause for Jesus' prediction in verse 2. Christian theologians fabricated the pronouncement in verse 2 after the demolition of the temple by the Romans in 70 CE. They commonly interpreted the demolition of the temple and the destruction of Jerusalem in retrospect as God's punishment of the Jews for rejecting and killing Jesus. Cf. Matt 22:7: "Then the king [= God] got angry and sent out his armies and killed these murderers and burned down their city."

8

In Jerusalem

Prediction of Judas' "Betrayal"

Mark 14:17–20

[17]And in the evening he comes with the Twelve.

[18]And when they were reclining at table eating, Jesus said, "Truly, I say to you, one of you who is eating with me will hand me over."

[19]They began to become sorrowful and to say to him, one after the other, "Is it I?"

[20]But he said to them, "One of the Twelve, who is dipping [the hand] with me in the dish."

ARGUMENT AGAINST AUTHENTICITY

Though Mark does not mention the name of Judas, he has him in mind. After verse 17 sets the scene, verses 18–20 employ an allusion to Ps 41:10—"Even my bosom friend in whom I trusted, who ate of my bread, has lifted the heel against me"—to announce Judas' hostile action and Jesus' foreknowledge of it.

Nonetheless it is wrong to say that Judas "betrayed" Jesus, as we can see from the history of the Judas tradition. First, and most critical, the Greek verb *paradidômi*, commonly translated as "to betray," should in fact be rendered as "to hand over" or "to deliver up." Second, the earliest extant account of Jesus' arrest appears in Paul's First Letter to the Corinthians, written about two decades before Mark. The account forms part of the Lord's Supper tradition, which Paul claims to have "received from the Lord" (1 Cor 11:23) about three years after the crucifixion, and subsequently transmitted to the Corinthian community during his first visit there (mid-first century). The traditional text begins: "The Lord Jesus, on the night when he was delivered up. . . ." Note, however, that at this stage, "delivering up" carries with it a theological significance that has nothing to do with the treachery of a scoundrel. Rather, it recalls the belief that, for the sake of Christian believers, God had made Jesus the true Suffering Servant from the Hebrew Bible Book of Isaiah—the servant punished by God for the salvation of the community (see esp. Isa 53:5–7). In fact, this interpretation dates from the earliest days of Paul's mission (mid-thirties) and permeates the earliest Christian confessions and should not be read into the story of Judas or the Last Supper.

Another point against such a misinterpretation is that Judas is listed as one of the Twelve. And it is this group—all twelve—who reportedly were the first to see the "risen" Jesus (1 Cor 15:5). This appearance is reported in a creedal formula (1 Cor 15:5) passed on to Paul immediately after his conversion and relayed by him to the Corinthian community during his first visit. Jesus founded this group of Twelve as a symbol of the imminent restitution of the Twelve tribes of Israel (Matt 19:28/Luke 22:28–30). Therefore, it is no wonder that the shock of Jesus' death led this same circle of followers, with Cephas (Peter) at its head, to witness the "risen" Jesus. In light of these observations, it is highly unlikely that Judas, being one of the Twelve, would have been identified in the earliest accounts as the "betrayer" of Jesus.

Later textual witnesses conform to the Gospel of Matthew (28:10) on this point, correcting Paul's writing by changing the appearance from "to the Twelve" to "to the Eleven." Similarly, in the Acts of the Apostles, Luke reports the election of a twelfth disciple to fill the place left empty by Judas (Acts 1:15–26). In both cases the harmonization is clearly intended to incorporate a secondary tradition of Judas as "betrayer."

It was not until early Christians tried to undergird the theological interpretation of the Passion story with "historical" details—partly to draw attention away from the embarrassing delay in Jesus' (Second) Coming—that they began to focus on an individual who may have connived in Jesus' arrest. They chose the disciple Judas, who presumably came from Kerioth in southern Judea. After all, no one could better symbolize the Jewish people (Judas/Judea/Jews), who had by then become the church's collective scapegoat and been assigned primary blame for Jesus' death. Thereafter, Jesus' salvific role as suffering Servant ("Jesus' blood shed for you") was forever distorted by a negative interpretation of the verb *paradidômi*: Judas was transformed from an eponymous symbol of the Twelve Tribes to a placard-bearing traitor, the Jew from Kerioth of Judea, and the Jews from God's chosen people to stylized personifications of evil. Authentic history is not to be found in such a convoluted smokescreen.

9

In Jerusalem
Predictions about the Actions
of the Disciples

Mark 14:27–30
*The disciples desert Jesus and Peter
thrice denies him*

²⁷"You will *all take offence*, for it is written,

> I will smite the shepherd
> and the sheep will be scattered. [Zech 13:7]

²⁸But after my resurrection I will go before you into Galilee."
²⁹And Peter said to him, "Though *all take offence*, I shall not!"
³⁰And Jesus says to him, "Truly, I tell you, today, this very
night, before the cock crows twice, you will deny me three
times."

ARGUMENT AGAINST AUTHENTICITY
Mark himself has formulated this scene long after the fact,
using a tradition that he will later develop in greater detail:
namely, that after Jesus was arrested, Peter repeatedly denied
knowing him (Mark 14:66–72).* Furthermore, in the report of Jesus' resurrection (Mark 16:1–8), verse 7 is such an
explicit reference to Mark 14:28 that the editorial character
of both verses is beyond question. As Mark's Son of God,
Jesus would naturally have had advance knowledge of these
two future events, as he did in the three announcements of
the passion and resurrection along with the prophecy of the

---

* The tradition of Peter's denial of Jesus must have an historical ker-
nel, namely that Peter distanced himself from his master during the
latter's arrest. The Christian community cannot have invented such an
action, because it would cast aspersions on the character of the first
leader of the church.

"betrayal" of Judas. The same is true of Jesus' prediction that the disciples would desert him, which in turn presupposes the flight that Mark later reports (Mark 14:50). It is significant that Mark supports this prediction of desertion in verse 27 with a scriptural quotation (Zech 13:7), for the first Christians dogmatically believed that everything related to Jesus happened according to the scriptures.

10

In Jerusalem
Answer to the High Priest

Mark 14:61b–62
Jesus' acknowledgement of divinity

[61b]Again the High Priest asked him and said to him, "Are you the Christ, the Son of the Most Blessed?"

[62]And Jesus said, "I am, and you will

> see the Son of man
> sitting on the right hand of Power and
> coming with the clouds of heaven." [cf. Dan 7:13;
> Ps 110:1]

ARGUMENT AGAINST AUTHENTICITY

These verses represent a compendium of Mark's view of Jesus as the Christ, the Son of God (1:11; 9:7; 15:39) *and* the Son of man (8:31; 9:31; 10:33). From the fact that Christological titles were ascribed to Jesus only after Easter, it follows that the above passage does not reproduce a real dialogue. Besides, the high priest would have never spoken of Jesus as the Son of God ("the most blessed") and Jesus would not have offered an affirmative self-characterization in response to a question that had not been asked.

11

In Jerusalem
Dialogue with Pilate

Mark 15:2
*Jesus' tacit acknowledgement to be
the King of the Jews*

And Pilate asked him, "Are you the King of the Jews?"
  And he answers and says to him, "You say so."

ARGUMENT AGAINST AUTHENTICITY

This invented dialogue stems from the probably factual report that Jesus was executed as "the King of the Jews"—that
is, as one who represented an actual or potential political
threat (cf. Mark 15:26). Pilate's question reflects the Roman
preoccupation with the disruptive effects of previous messianic pretenders (cf. Theudas and Judas the Galilean; Acts
5:36–37), and it echoes the fabricated messianic confession
of Jesus before the Supreme Council (Mark 14:62).

John 18:33–37
*Jesus proclaims himself a King born
to bear witness to the truth*

[33]Now Pilate again went into the praetorium and called Jesus and
said to him, "Are you the KING of the *Jews?*"
  [34]Jesus answered, "Do you say this of your own accord, or
have others said it to you about me?"
  [35]Pilate answered, "Am I a *Jew?* Your people and the chief
priests have *delivered* you *up* to me. What have you done?"
  [36]Jesus answered, "My KINGDOM is not of this world. If my
KINGDOM were of this world, my servants would have fought,
that I might not be *delivered up* to the *Jews.* But as it is, my
KINGDOM is not an earthly one."
  [37]Then Pilate said to him, "So you are a KING?"

Jesus answered, "It is you who say I am a KING, but it is this I was born for, and this is why I have come into the world—to bear witness to the **truth**. Every one who lives according to the **truth** hears my voice."

ARGUMENT AGAINST AUTHENTICITY

The first direct encounter in John between Pilate and Jesus takes place here (verse 33). The question, "Are you the King of the Jews?" corresponds to Mark 15:2a and no doubt similarly reflects the perceived threat of a political claim on the part of Jesus. Jesus' counter-question in verse 34 challenges Pilate to be clear as to the nature of and motive for his implicit charge. Pilate claims to have no cause of his own to proceed against Jesus (verse 35). Indeed, the fact that he has to ask the *accused* what guilt he has incurred is likely intended to show that he has allowed the Jews to force him into the position of judge. Only now (verse 36) does Jesus begin to answer the question in verse 33. That he first speaks of his kingdom in negative terms must reassure Pilate. If Jesus' kingdom is "not of this world" (cf. John 8:23) and if moreover he has no earthly means of power (cf. Matt. 26:53), there is no occasion for the Roman authorities to proceed against him. Verse 37 continues: Jesus is indeed a king ("It is you who say it" corresponds to Mark 15:2b parr.), but he makes no political claims. Rather, he has come into this world (cf. John 6:14; 11:27) to bear witness to the truth (cf. John 8:40, 45; see also 5:33). For the last sentence of Jesus' answer cf. John 8:47.

The entire dialogue is a fencing match contrived by the author of the Fourth Gospel to showcase a number of doctrinal and polemical ideas.

12

In Jerusalem

Words on the Cross

Mark 15:34

Quotation of Psalm 22:2

"My God, my God (Aramaic *Elohi, Elohi*), why have you forsaken me?"

ARGUMENT AGAINST AUTHENTICITY

Jesus' complaint corresponds word for word with Ps 22:2 with the exception that, there, God is addressed in Hebrew as *Eli*, whereas Mark has the Aramaic *Elohi*. Although Jesus spoke Aramaic, the very fact that Mark gave the cry in its Aramaic version is an argument against its historicity. It is impossible for the Roman soldiers to have heard the words *Elohi*, etc., handed down in Aramaic, as a prayer to Elijah, as is reported in Mark 15:35: "And some of the bystanders hearing it said, 'Look, he is calling Elijah'."

But there cannot be other witnesses other than the soldiers, since the women are said to have observed Jesus' death on the cross only from a distance (Mark 15:40–41), assuming this note has any historical value. Finally, two other reasons argue against the historicity of this cry of Jesus from the cross. *First*, contradictory prayers of Jesus on the cross have been handed down (see below). *Second*, the primitive Christian mind longed for adorning the crucifixion scene with borrowings from the Hebrew Bible. Psalms 22, 31 and 69 provided most of the material for these borrowings (see below, p. 112).

It was edifying to read the passion story in the light of the Psalter. This custom helped to overcome the offensive scenario that God's Son, who was daily present in worship, had had to drink the bitter cup of death.

Matthew 27:46
Quotation of Mark 15:34
"My God, My God (Hebrew *Eli, Eli*), why have you forsaken me?"

ARGUMENT AGAINST AUTHENTICITY
Matthew presupposes Mark 15:34 and changes "Elohi" into "Eli." In so doing, he is taking account of the biblical basis in Ps 22:2 and explaining why the Roman soldiers could have heard Jesus' cry as a cry to Elijah. The historicity of this cry can be ruled out because Matthew used Mark's inauthentic report (15:34) and was not himself an eyewitness.

Luke 23:34a
Forgiveness of the perpetrators
"Father, forgive them; for they do not know what they are doing."

ARGUMENT AGAINST AUTHENTICITY
Luke's account of the crucifixion has no recognized sources other than the Gospel of Mark. This means that we must regard any difference from Mark's account as a Lukan redaction, that all three sayings of Jesus on the cross (Luke 23:34a, 43b, and 46b) derive from his pen, and that Mark 15:34 has been purposely omitted.

Also of interest is the fact that Luke 23:34a is lacking in a number of important ancient manuscripts. It has been either eliminated there or deliberately inserted here to parallel the cry of the dying Stephen in Acts 7:60: "Lord, do not hold this sin against them!"

Luke 23:43
Promise to one of the criminals on the cross
"Truly, I say to you, today you will be with me in paradise."

ARGUMENT AGAINST AUTHENTICITY
This verse constitutes Jesus' reply to the request of one of the two men who were crucified with him (verse 42: "Jesus,

remember me when you come into your kingdom") and clearly presupposes the notion Jesus' immediate ascension. Evidently the saying represents an attempt to overcome the problem of the delay of the Second Coming of Jesus: contrary to the earliest Christian expectation, Jesus' disciples need not wait for their heavenly reward until the end of the present age, but will receive it immediately after death. Luke did not care about the contradiction between the ascent of Jesus from the cross and his ascent on Easter Day in 24:51. Naturally, if the saying is indissolubly bound up with the delay of the second Coming, it cannot possibly be historical.

Luke 23:46
Quotation of Psalm 31:6
"Father, into your hands I commend my spirit."

ARGUMENT AGAINST AUTHENTICITY
The sentence corresponds to Ps 31:6 and derives from the early Christian tendency to interpret the passion of Jesus in the light of Hebrew Bible psalms. The content of this prayer contradicts Mark 15:34, itself a quotation from a Hebrew Bible psalm, that Luke has replaced by a citation from Ps 31:6 in order to show that Jesus was strong until the very end. The author's editorial shenanigans indicate a fictional result.

John 19:25–27
The beloved disciple designated as Jesus' successor

²⁵Now standing by the cross of Jesus were his **mother**, and his **mother**'s sister, Mary the wife of Clopas, and Mary Magdalene.

²⁶When Jesus saw his **mother**, and THE DISCIPLE WHOM HE LOVED standing near, he said to (his) **mother**, "Woman, look, your son!"

²⁷Then he said to THE DISCIPLE, "Look, your **mother**!"

And from that hour THE DISCIPLE took her to his own home.

ARGUMENT AGAINST AUTHENTICITY

In view of the precise enumeration of the women in verse 25 (which surprisingly includes the mother of Jesus, who is not mentioned at this point by the other three New Testament Gospels), it is striking that according to verses 26–27 the Beloved Disciple, who in the passion narrative had not previously been mentioned, was also standing by the cross. John has created this otherwise inexplicable grouping by connecting it with Jesus' last hours and thereby has dramatized an element from the tradition (verses 26–27) that dealt with the bond between Mary and the Beloved Disciple, but which originally had nothing to do with the death of Jesus.

The scene cannot lay any claim to historicity. For one thing, in Mark 15:40–41 (Matt 27:55; Luke 23:49) the women observe what is happening on the cross *from afar*. For another, no other report places either Jesus' mother or any of the disciples with the women near the cross.

John 19:30
God's mission fulfilled

"It is finished!"

ARGUMENT AGAINST AUTHENTICITY

According to the Fourth Gospel's theological concept, the passion of Jesus is the completion of the mission of the Son of God. Through his death on the cross he returns to the glory he had from the very beginning as the Pre-existent One (cf. John 1). John can even say that the crucifixion of Jesus is identical with his exaltation to the Father (cf. John 3:14; 8:28) or his glorification (cf. John 12:23, 28; 13:31–32; 17:1, 5). It is in keeping with this that even on the cross Jesus remains the Lord who is in command, unbroken and unshaken. For this reason the evangelist suppresses any cry of despair or forsakenness and instead makes Jesus utter the triumphant saying "It is finished." Since the saying derives from John's overall theological conception, it is clearly inauthentic.

13

In Jerusalem
Words at the Empty Tomb

John 20:17
The charge to Mary Magdalene

Jesus says to her, "Do not touch me, for I have not yet *ascended* to the FATHER. But go to my brothers and tell them, 'I am *ascending* to my FATHER and your FATHER, to my GOD and your GOD'."

ARGUMENT AGAINST AUTHENTICITY

The "Risen One"—not the historical Jesus—speaks, and tells specifically of a non-historical event: his ascension to God (see John 3:13; 6:62).

Matthew 28:10
The charge to the two Marys

Then Jesus said to them, "Do not be afraid! Go and proclaim to my brothers that they are to go to Galilee. There they will see me."

ARGUMENT AGAINST AUTHENTICITY

Again it is the "Risen One" who speaks, and here simply repeats what the angel at the tomb has already said: "Do not be afraid! . . . Go quickly and tell his disciples that he has been raised from the dead. And look, he will go before you to Galilee; there you will see him" (Matt 28:5–7). This is simply didactic reiteration on the author's part.

14

In Galilee

Charge to Peter

John 21:15–19

[15]When they had finished breakfast,
Jesus says to Simon Peter, "Simon son of John, DO YOU LOVE ME
more than these?"

He says to him, "Yes **LORD**, YOU KNOW THAT I LOVE YOU."
He says to him, "*Feed* my lambs."

[16]He says to him, a second time, "Simon son of John, DO YOU
LOVE ME?"

He says to him, "Yes, **LORD**, YOU KNOW THAT I LOVE YOU."
Jesus says to him, "Tend my SHEEP."

[17]He says to him the third time, "Simon son of John, DO YOU
LOVE ME?"

Peter was grieved because he said to him the third time, "DO
YOU LOVE ME?" And he says to him, "**LORD**, you know everything; YOU KNOW THAT I LOVE YOU."

Jesus says to him, "*Feed* my SHEEP.
[18]Truly, truly, I say to you,
when you were young,
you *girded* yourself
and walked where you wanted.
But when you are old,
you will stretch out your hands, and another will *gird* you
and take you where you do not want (to go)."
[19a]He said this to show by what death he was to glorify God.
[19b]And after he had said this he tells him, "Follow me!"

ARGUMENT AGAINST AUTHENTICITY
Here the Evangelist has the "Risen One" commission Peter
as the leader of the church universal while at the same time
prophesying his martyrdom.

This section is loosely linked with the preceding one by the note "when they had finished breakfast," which points back to John 21:12–13. Its purpose is to present an emphatic restoration of Peter's honor, which had been seriously compromised by his denial of Jesus.

The direct and indirect references to John 1:42; 10:1–8; 13:36–38 and 18:17, 25–27 show that this scene has been created with a theological purpose: namely, to derive from the Risen One Peter's leading position in the church—one that he holds despite his earlier denial of his Lord (cf. Matt 16:17–19; Luke 22:32).

Verses 15–17 have a unitary structure. Three times Jesus asks Peter, the son of John (cf. John 1:42), whether he loves him, and three times Peter confirms his devotion. Each time his answer is followed by a command of Jesus appointing him shepherd of the sheep, i.e., the leader of the church (note the appended qualification in John 10:1–18). Peter's thrice-repeated affirmation corresponds to this threefold denial in the courtyard of the high priest (John 18:17, 25–27), and Peter is exonerated from his heavy guilt by the thrice-repeated charge.

The third exchange of words is continued in verse 18: Jesus predicts Peter's martyrdom, i.e. he formulates a *vaticinium ex eventu* (Peter had already died when verse 18 was written; cf. 1 Clement 5:2–4 dating from 97 C.E.).

The commentary made in verse 19a on the basis of John 12:33 or 18:32 says that Peter's particular kind of death is a special mark of distinction for him. It is evidently assumed that he, too, was crucified.

In verse 19b Jesus extends the charge to lead and protect the community by an invitation to personal discipleship, which because of verses 18–19a is also to be understood as a call to discipleship extending into martyrdom (cf. John 13:36).

In sum, every sentence in this passage is fabricated.

INAUTHENTIC SAYINGS OF JESUS IN THE NEW TESTAMENT GOSPELS

Topics of Jesus' Preaching

15

Against External Enemies
Israel and Its Leaders

Mark 12:1b–11

*The wicked tenants, or Jewish leaders
punished for murdering Jesus*

[1b]A man planted a *vineyard*, and set a hedge around it, and dug a pit for the winepress, and built a tower, and let it out to TENANTS, and traveled away.

[2]And he SENT to the TENANTS a *servant* at the appointed time so that he might receive from the TENANTS part of the fruit of the *vineyard*. [3]And they seized him, BEAT him and SENT him away empty-handed.

[4]And again he SENT to them another *servant*: him too they struck on the head and treated shamefully.

[5]And he SENT another. They even **killed** that one and many others, some they BEAT, others they **killed**.

[6]He still had one other, a beloved *SON*. He SENT him to them last, saying, "They will respect my *SON*." [7]But the TENANTS said to one another, "This is the heir. Up, let us **kill** him, and the inheritance will belong to us." [8]So they took him and **killed** him, and threw him out of the *vineyard*.

[9]What then will the LORD of the *vineyard* do? He will come and destroy the TENANTS and give the *vineyard* to others.

[10]Do you not know this scripture,

> The stone that the builders rejected has become the
> cornerstone;
> [11]the LORD has done this,
> and it is marvelous in our eyes? [Ps 118:22–23]

ARGUMENT AGAINST AUTHENTICITY
The text is a Markan allegory based on the song of the vineyard in Isa 5:1–7. In an allegory the true understanding of the story as a whole is achieved only by transferring all its

essential elements to another frame of reference. In the present text, for example, each of the main elements stands for something else:

The vineyard (verse 1) represents Israel; the tenants (verse 1) are its leaders; the owner of the land (verse 1) is God; the servants (verses 2–5) are the Jewish prophets; the only beloved son (verse 6) and heir (verse 7) is Christ; the killing of the son (verse 8) refers to the murder of Jesus; the punishment of the tenants (verse 9) stands for the rejection of Israel; and "others" (verse 9) refers to the Gentile church.

The point of the allegory is that because the Jewish leaders have murdered Jesus, they themselves will be killed and God's promise to Israel will be bestowed upon the Gentiles. In order to confirm that by scriptural proof, Ps 118:22–23 is added in verses 10–11. The image used here, that of the rejected stone that God has made the corner stone of the Temple, was a popular proof text in the early church for the resurrection of the Christ rejected by the Jews (cf. Acts 4:11; 1 Pet 2:4, 6–8).

Clearly, then, this tradition derives from the community, and the historical Jesus cannot have been the speaker. Besides, Jesus did not speak in allegories but in parables, a narrative form that avoids multiple points of comparison. (Cf. below, pp. 90–93.)

Matthew 22:2–14

The allegory of the wedding feast

²The kingdom of heaven is like a *king* who prepared a *wedding* for his son.

³And he sent his SLAVES to call **those who were invited** to the *wedding*, but they did not want to come.

⁴Again he sent out other SLAVES and said, "Tell **those who are invited**, 'Look, I have prepared my banquet, my oxen and my fat calves have been slaughtered, and all is ready; come to the *wed-*

ding.'" ⁵But they scorned (the reminder) and went away, one to his own field, the other to his business. ⁶And the rest seized his SLAVES, treated them shamefully and killed them.

⁷Then the **king** grew angry and sent out his armies and put to death these murderers and burned down their city.

⁸Then he said to his SLAVES, "The *wedding* is ready, but **those invited** were not worthy. ⁹Therefore go out into the thoroughfares and **invite** whomever you find to the *wedding*." ¹⁰ᵃAnd the SLAVES went out onto the streets and gathered together all whom they found, ¹⁰ᵇbad and good; and the *wedding* was filled with GUESTS.

[Secondary interpretation:] ¹¹But when the **king** came in to look at his GUESTS, he saw a man *without a wedding garment.* ¹²And he says to him, "Friend, how did you get in here *without wedding garment?*" But he fell silent. ¹³Then the **king** said to the servants, "Bind him hand and foot, and throw him into the darkness outside, where there will be weeping and gnashing of teeth."

[Additional secondary interpretation:] ¹⁴"For many are **invited**, but few are **chosen**."

ARGUMENT AGAINST AUTHENTICITY

The text consists of three units:

(a) Verses 2–10 are an allegory of salvation history extending to the period after Easter. The king, i.e. God, arranges a wedding celebration for his son, namely Jesus Christ, and sends his slaves to invite the Jews to participate. The first group of slaves (verse 3) stands for the prophets and the repudiation of their message; the second group (verse 4) denotes the apostles and missionaries sent to Israel (Jerusalem) and the maltreatment and martyrdom that some of them suffered (verse 6). They invite the Jews to enter the kingdom of God by their preaching of the gospel, but come up against indifference among the upper classes. Sending out into the streets (verses 9–10) suggests the mission to the Gentiles, and the entry into the wedding hall (verse 10b) baptism. The vivid statement in verse 7 reflects an intensification of anti-Judaism: the murderous Jews are put to death and their city, Jerusalem, is set on fire—the latter a retrospective allusion to the destruction of Jerusalem in 70 CE. With "bad and good" in verse 10b, Matthew prepares for verses 11–14 which follow.

(b) Verses 11–13, which are likely a fragment of a separate parable the original form of which cannot be reconstructed, inculcate the role of good works and emphasize that Matthew is concerned with moral conduct lest verse 9, which relates the indiscriminate invitation of guests, give the impression of indifference on ethical matters. For "weeping and gnashing of teeth" (verse 13) see Matt 8:12; 13:42; 13:50; 24:51; 25:30.

(c) In verse 14 Matthew inserts a logion from the tradition in order to comment on the whole passage, here verses 2–13. Certainly many are invited from Israel and the Gentiles, but only a few are chosen to be saved. Unfortunately, this saying contradicts both verses 11–13 and verses 2–10, because in verses 11–13 only a single guest is expelled, and in verses 2–10 not a single individual accepts the invitation.

Not only does the exaggerated and grossly anti-Jewish allegory reflect a recurring animus of the First Evangelist, but the clear allusion to the destruction of Jerusalem, which occurred some forty years after Jesus' death, also makes it obvious that Jesus cannot have told this tale.

Matthew 23:13–36
Woes against the scribes and Pharisees

[1] ¹³"WOE TO YOU, SCRIBES AND PHARISEES, *YOU HYPOCRITES*! You shut the kingdom of heaven in people's faces. You yourselves do not enter, nor will you let those enter who are trying to.*

---

* Matt 23:14 reads, "Woe to you, scribes and Pharisees, hypocrites! For you devour widows' houses and for a pretense you make long prayers. Therefore you will receive the greater condemnation." It does not belong to the original text and is not part of the oldest manuscripts.

[2] ¹⁵"**WOE TO YOU, SCRIBES AND PHARISEES,** *YOU HYPO-CRITES*! You traverse sea and land to make a single proselyte, and when he becomes (one), you make him a child of **HELL** twice (as bad) as yourselves.

[3] ¹⁶"**WOE TO YOU, BLIND GUIDES**, who say,

> If anyone *SWEARS* by the TEMPLE, it means nothing;
> but if anyone *SWEARS* by the GOLD of the TEMPLE, **he is bound by his oath**.

^{17a}Foolish and BLIND (people)!

^{17b}<u>Which is greater: the GOLD, or the TEMPLE that makes the gold sacred?</u>

¹⁸"Or,

> If anyone *SWEARS* by the *ALTAR*, it means nothing;
> but if anyone *SWEARS* by the *gift* on it, **he is bound by his oath**.

^{19a}BLIND (people) that you are!

^{19b}<u>Which is greater: the *gift*, or the *ALTAR* that makes the *gift* sacred?</u>

> ²⁰So whoever *SWEARS* by the *ALTAR*,
> *SWEARS* by it and by everything on it.
> ²¹And whoever *SWEARS* by the TEMPLE,
> *SWEARS* by it and by him who inhabits it.
> ²²And whoever *SWEARS* by heaven,
> *SWEARS* by the throne of God and by the one who sits on it.

[4] ²³"**WOE TO YOU, SCRIBES AND PHARISEES,** *YOU HYPO-CRITES*, for you tithe mint and dill and cumin, and have neglected the weightier matters of the law: justice and mercy and faith. It is these you ought to have followed without neglecting the former. ²⁴You BLIND GUIDES, straining out a gnat and swallowing a camel!

[5] ²⁵"**WOE TO YOU, SCRIBES AND PHARISEES,** *YOU HYPO-CRITES*, for you cleanse the outside of the cup and of the plate, but inside they are full of extortion and rapacity. ²⁶You BLIND Pharisee, first cleanse the inside of the cup and of the plate, that the outside also may be *clean*.

[6] ²⁷"**WOE TO YOU, SCRIBES AND PHARISEES,** *YOU HYPO-CRITES*, for you are like whitewashed tombs, which outwardly

appear beautiful but within are filled with the bones of the dead and all manner of *uncleanness*. [28]So you also outwardly appear RIGHTEOUS to people, but within you are full of *HYPOCRISY* and iniquity.

[7] [29]"WOE TO YOU, SCRIBES AND PHARISEES, *YOU HYPO-CRITES*, for you build tombs for the prophets and adorn the graves of the RIGHTEOUS [30]and say, "If we had lived in the days of **our fathers**, we would not have taken part with them in shedding the blood of the *PROPHETS*." [31]Thus you witness against yourselves that you are sons of those who murdered the *PROPH-ETS*. [32]Fill up, then, the measure of **your fathers**! [33]You serpents, you brood of vipers, how are you to escape being sentenced to **HELL?**

[34]"Therefore, look, I send you *PROPHETS* and sages and SCRIBES; and (some) of them you will kill and crucify; and (some) you will scourge in your synagogues and persecute from town to town, [35]that upon you may come all the RIGHTEOUS blood shed on earth, from the blood of Abel the RIGHTEOUS to the blood of Zechariah the son of Barachiah, whom you murdered between the sanctuary and the altar [cf. 2 Chron 24:20–22]. [36]Truly, I say to you, all this will come upon this generation."

ARGUMENT AGAINST AUTHENTICITY

This is a part of a speech that Matthew attributes to Jesus (23:2–39), but is his creation even more obviously than the Sermon on the Mount (5:3–7:27). The First Evangelist uses Mark's warning against the scribes (Mark 12:37c–40 = Matt 23:1–2a, 6–7) to anchor the discourse in the Markan narra-tive and elaborates the harangue using Q (Luke 11:37–52; 13:34–35). He leaves the speech in the context he found in Mark 12:38–40; but here the scribe, who in Mark was not far from the kingdom of God (Mark 12:34), has become a mere tempter (Matt 22:35)—a gloomy appetizer for the fire, brimstone and pitch that Matthew's Jesus will pour on the scribes and Pharisees.

Seven woes brand the scribes and the Pharisees as hypocrites (Matt 23:13–33). Seven is a symbolic number indicating completeness and is meant to further intensify the force of the charges.

As Matthew found only six woes in the tradition, he composed the third woe (Matt 23:16–22), as is evident from the somewhat different introduction. Besides, the third woe is lengthier than any of the other six. Its first part (verses 16–19) has a parallel structure and, by giving various examples, makes a single point: it is absurd to maintain that an oath sworn by what is lesser is not binding, while to swear by what is greater creates a binding commitment. The second part of the third woe (verses 20–22) draws the conclusion: whether one swears by the temple, the gold of the temple, the altar, the gift on the altar, or by heaven, the oath is binding. Since this debate over the validity of oaths presupposes the existence of the temple, the tradition behind this passage must predate its destruction by the Romans in 70 CE. Yet its content is almost certainly to be derived from a Christian tradition and not from the historical Jesus, who taught his followers to refrain from oaths (Matt 5:34), and, as one who enjoined love of enemies (Matt 5:44a/Luke 6:27), can hardly be imagined to have indulged in such a spate of vituperation.

As their similar style shows, the other six woes derive from the same layer of tradition and received the same introductory formula from Matthew. They are characterized by hostility to the religious leaders of Judaism. The explanation of their harsh polemic may be that these reflect controversies within an association of synagogues that had become partly Christian. In verse 13 the scribes and Pharisees are made a negative counterpart of Peter: they shut the door to the Kingdom of Heaven instead of opening it, as was said of Peter in Matt 16:19a. Verse 15 is a reflection of Jewish missionary activity.

Whereas the preaching of judgment up to verse 33 applied only to the scribes and Pharisees, in verses 34–36 the formal address to the scribes and Pharisees is omitted in order also to hint at their successors after the destruction of Jerusalem. The prophets, sages, and scribes of verse 34 represent Christian leaders of Matthew's own day. Some of them will suffer the fate of being killed, crucified, and scourged (cf. Matt 10:17; 22:6) at the hands of the scribes and Pharisees, who are to be held responsible, and liable to punishment, for "all the righteous blood shed on earth" (verse 35). Besides, as verse 36 shows, Matthew is thinking of a judgment on all Israel, the announcement of which he puts into Jesus' mouth. With this he has reached the goal of the whole passage.

John 8:37–45
The unbelieving Jews as the
offspring of the devil

[37]"I know that you are the seed of *Abraham*; yet YOU SEEK TO KILL ME, for my word finds no place in you. [38]I speak of what I have understood from the FATHER, but YOU DO NOT DO WHAT YOU HAVE HEARD FROM THE FATHER."

[39]They answered him, "Our FATHER is *Abraham*."

Jesus says to them, "If you were *Abraham*'s children, you would do the works of *Abraham*, [40]but now YOU SEEK TO KILL ME, a person who has told you the TRUTH which he has heard from GOD. *Abraham* did not do this. [41]YOU DO THE WORKS OF YOUR FATHER."

They said to him, "We were not born of fornication; we have one FATHER, GOD."

[42]Jesus said to them, "If GOD were your FATHER, you would love me, for I proceeded from GOD and have come; for I came not of my own accord, but he sent me.

[43]"Why do you not understand my speech? Because you cannot hear my word. [44]You are of (your) FATHER, (who is) the devil, and you want to do your FATHER's desires. He was a murderer

from the beginning, and did not stand in the **TRUTH**, because there is no **TRUTH** in him. When he speaks *LIES*, he speaks from his own, for he is a *LIAR* and a **FATHER** of *LIES*.

⁴⁵"But I—because I speak the **TRUTH**, you do not believe me."

ARGUMENT AGAINST AUTHENTICITY

The Jesus of this text calls the Jews who do not believe in him children of the devil. This illustrates the extreme bitterness of the conflict between Johannine Christians and their Jewish neighbors. His reproach of the Jews, "You seek to kill me" (verse 37) runs like a scarlet thread through the Fourth Gospel (see John 5:18; 7:1, 19–20, 25). Without doubt this acrimony can be explained by conflicts between members of Johannine congregations and unconverted Jews. In that respect, of course, the views we find here were the product of their time; nonetheless, the author is convinced of what he puts into Jesus' mouth, and he clearly intends to demonize the Jews. This action need not indicate a significant theological distance between them and the Johannine community; indeed, it may well bear witnesses to a controversy within Judaism that only later culminated in a final separation. Clashes between groups that retain some common bond are always nastier than those between parties who have little interest in each other. None of this, of course, mitigates the venom of the denunciations proclaimed.

Obviously the unbelieving Jews play a significant role in the framework of Johannine dualism, with its contrasts between God and the world, light and darkness, truth and lie. As representatives of the world, Jews become allegorical stand-ins for any who do not believe. They represent the darkness (John 8:12), the lie (John 8:44), and death (John 8:51). They are "of this world" and come "from below" (John 8:23). Since they have not confessed the one who comes "from above" but is not "of this world," they must die in their sins (John 8:24). They neither know God (John

7:28; 8:55; 15:21; 16:3), nor can they know him, for God can be known only through the Son (John 7:29). Because they judge "according to the flesh" (John 8:15), they remain in bondage, for only through the Son can people be really free (John 8:32–36).

Attributing this hate-filled vituperation to Jesus, who as a true Jew proclaimed love of God and neighbor to be the essence of the law (Mark 12:28–31), should be sufficient evidence of its inauthenticity.

The other side of this uncompromising hostility to the unbelieving Jews lies in John's understanding of Christ; this we can see, for example, in John 14:6: "I am the way and the truth and the life; no one comes to the Father, but by me." This saying will be shown to be inauthentic; see below, p. 108.

16

Against Internal Enemies
Liberal and Enthusiastic Christians

Matthew 5:17–19
Unrestricted validity of the law

¹⁷"Do not think that I have come TO ABOLISH the **law** or the prophets; I have not come TO ABOLISH but to fulfill.

¹⁸"For truly, I say to you, till heaven and earth *pass away*, not the smallest stroke nor a dot in the **law** will *pass away*, until all is fulfilled.

¹⁹"Whoever now ABOLISHES one of the least of these commandments and *teaches* people so will be called the least *in the kingdom of heaven*; but whoever does and *teaches* [it] will be called great *in the kingdom of heaven*."

ARGUMENT AGAINST AUTHENTICITY

Verse 17 derives from Matthew in its entirety. The beginning corresponds to the introduction in Matt 10:34, which similarly stems from Matthew. "Fulfill" is one of the First Evangelist's favorite words. The phrase "law and prophets" is also attested as Matthean by its appearance in Matt 7:12 and 22:40. In principle, "fulfill" has a positive significance, as also emerges from the contrast with "annul." In verse 17 Matthew may be correcting a saying falsely attributed to Jesus that he regards as counterfeit: e.g., "I have come to abolish the law and the prophets." In this matter, note the stringent reinterpretations of the law in the subsequent verses 21–48 and compare with Matt 13:41, where Matthew's interpretation of the parable of the weeds harshly condemns all sinners and evildoers—people from whom such a "false" saying of Jesus could come. Verse 18 substantiates the statement of verse 17 and is characterized by the same positive attitude to the law. "The least of these commandments" (verse 19) refers to the traditional teachings presented by Jesus from Matt 5:21 to 7:21. At any rate, since the issues involved in this passage reflect a Christian community many years after the death of Jesus, the words cannot be his.

Matthew 7:13–23
*The necessity of fully observing the law
and doing the will of God even under
difficult circumstances*

13"Enter through the narrow *gate*.

"For wide is the *gate* and smooth is the ROAD THAT LEADS TO destruction, and many enter through it.

"14But narrow is the *gate* and rough the ROAD THAT LEADS TO life, and only a few find it."

15"Watch out for false prophets. They come to you in sheep's clothing, but inwardly they are ferocious wolves. 16a*By their* **fruits** *you shall know them*.

"16bDo people pick grapes from thornbushes, or figs from thistles?

"17Likewise every *good tree* bears good **fruits**, but a bad tree bears bad **fruits**.

"18A *good tree* cannot bear bad **fruits**, and a bad tree cannot bear good **fruits**. 19Every tree that does not bear good **fruit** is cut down and thrown into the fire. 20Thus, *by their* **fruits** *you shall know them*."

21"Not everyone who says to me, "LORD, LORD," will enter the kingdom of heaven, but only the one who does the will of my Father who is in heaven.

22"Many will say to me on that day,

LORD, LORD, did we not prophesy IN YOUR NAME?

Did we not IN YOUR NAME drive out demons?

Did we not IN YOUR NAME perform many miracles?

23Then I will tell them plainly,

I never knew you.

Away from me, you evildoers!" [Ps 6:9 LXX]

ARGUMENT AGAINST AUTHENTICITY

Verses 13–14 derive from Matthew. The way through the narrow gate that leads to life is the way of righteousness defined by the instructions of the Sermon on the Mount. Matthew formulates verse 15 as a prelude to what follows and adds verse 16a as a transition repeated in verse 20 to round off the unit consisting of verses 16–20. Verses 16b–18 (cf. Thomas 45:1–2) partly correspond to the Q parable of the tree with the fruits and its application to a person's speech (cf. Luke 6:43–45). This parable appears more completely in Matt 12:33–35. In verse 19 Jesus repeats part of John the Baptist's preaching (Matt 3:10/Luke 3:9). Hence I infer that also verses 17–18, which have the same topic (tree/fruits), have been derived from verse 19. Notice that elsewhere Matthew similarly attributes the same teaching to John the Baptist and Jesus (Matt 3:2 and 4:17). The warning in verse 21 offers an advance summary of verses 22–23, which are directed against "false" prophets in Matthew's community.

The section is stamped throughout by Matthew's purpose and the problems in his communities. With the possible exception of verse 16b, it is his invention.

John 5:28–29
Resurrection to life and to judgment

[28]"Do not marvel at this; for the hour is coming when all who are in the tombs will hear his [the Son's] voice

[29]and those who have done good will come forth for the resurrection of life,

but those who have done evil to the resurrection of judgment."

ARGUMENT AGAINST AUTHENTICITY

John 5:24 stresses that every believer already partakes of eternal life. It reads: "Truly, truly, I say to you, whoever hears my words and believes in him who has sent me has eternal life and does not come into judgment, but has passed from death to life." This verse is a key formulation by the Fourth Evangelist. As in John 6:47 and 11:25–26, he sums up his new interpretation of the traditional eschatology. Salvation and doom are not decided at the end of days, but in the present. Thus, the traditional eschatology becomes a realized eschatology. As John 3:18b (the negative versions of verse 24) shows, realized eschatology also entails a threat: "Whoever does not believe in me, has been judged already."

In other words, the popular teaching about the personal salvation that was replaced in verse 24 is reestablished in verses 28–29 by later revisers who did not like the sole emphasis on the presence of salvation. And since all this formulating and reformulating is going on long after Jesus' death, it cannot be assigned to him.

John 6:51c–58

Realistic understanding of the Eucharist

51c[Jesus:] "And the bread which I will give is my flesh for the life of the world."

52Then the Jews disputed among themselves, saying, "How can this man give us his flesh to eat?" 53Then Jesus said to them, "Truly, truly, I say to you, unless you eat the flesh of the Son of man and drink his blood, you have no life in you.

54"*ANYONE WHO CHEWS MY FLESH AND DRINKS MY BLOOD* has eternal life, and I will raise him up at the last day. 55For my flesh is real food and my blood is real drink.

56"*ANYONE WHO CHEWS MY FLESH AND DRINKS MY BLOOD* remains in me, and I in him.

57"As the living Father has sent me, and I live through the Father, so anyone who *CHEWS* me will live through me.

58"This is the **bread** which came down from heaven, not as the fathers ate and have died. Anyone who *CHEWS this* **bread** will live forever."

ARGUMENT AGAINST AUTHENTICITY

This passage emphasizes the necessity of the Eucharist for salvation. This fact alone is puzzling because elsewhere the Fourth Gospel is evidently indifferent to cultic sacramental piety, if not critical of it. For example, in John's account of Jesus' last supper (John 13), the institution of the Eucharist is not mentioned. Besides, this passage represents an alien body in the context of chapter 6:

(a) In John 6:51a, Jesus is identical with the "bread that came down from heaven" (cf. John 6:35, 41, 48); according to verse 51c the bread is his flesh. Here there is as little preparation for this identification in John 6:31–51b as there is for the mention of blood (verses 53–55), which now additionally comes into play.

(b) According to John 6:32 it is the *Father* who *gives* (present tense) the bread; according to verse 51c it is Jesus who *will give* (future tense) the bread.

(c) "Bread" and "eat" evidently have a symbolic meaning in verses John 6:32–51b: Jesus is the "bread" of which one is to "eat" by faith (verse 51b). By contrast, in verses 51c–58 "bread" (or "flesh"), "eat", "blood," and "drink" are meant in a real sense: here, consumption of the flesh and blood of Jesus is called for. In the original Greek, the use of the verb *trôgein* "chew" instead of *esthiein* or *phagein* "eat" reinforces the literal understanding.

(d) In John 6:33, 35, 40, 47–51b life is promised to the one who believes; according to John 6:51c–58 the gift of life is bound up with the sacrificial consumption of the flesh and blood of Jesus, and no mention of faith is made.

(e) Whereas in verses 51c–58 the flesh is regarded as a saving gift, according to verse 63 it is of no use.

Evidently, the passage at issue was added to the Fourth Gospel by later revisers. The understanding of the Eucharist that these theologians share matches that of bishop Ignatius of Antioch (early second century), who regarded the Eucharist as a "poison against death" or as "a drug of immortality" (Eph 20:2).

17

Prophecies about the Judgment

Matthew 23:37–39
Lament over Jerusalem

37"Jerusalem, Jerusalem, you who kill the prophets and stone those who are sent to you! How often would I have gathered your children together as a hen gathers her brood under her wings, but you were unwilling! 38Look, your house will be left desolate for you. 39aFor I tell you, you will not see me again until you say,

39bBlessed is he who comes in the name of the Lord."
[Ps 118:26]

ARGUMENT AGAINST AUTHENTICITY

The lament over Jerusalem presupposes the knowledge of its destruction in the Jewish War (67–70 CE). Jesus will be returning as judge of the world (verse 39b), but all hope will have been lost; and when the scribes, Pharisees, and hostile Jews will be forced to greet him, it will be too late. Jesus is being made to foresee what the writer knows by experience (destruction of Jerusalem) and by faith (Jesus' return as a judge).

Luke 23:27–31
Lament over the inhabitants of Jerusalem

27And there followed him a large number of people and women, who bewailed and lamented him.

28But Jesus turned to them and said, "Daughters of Jerusalem, do not weep for me; weep for yourselves and for your children. 29For look, the time will come when they say,

Blessed are the barren,
and the wombs that never gave birth
and the breasts that never gave suck! [cf. Isa 54:1]

³⁰Then they will begin

> to say to the mountains,
> Fall on us!
> and to the hills,
> Cover us! [Hos 10:8]

³¹For if they do this when the wood is green, what will happen when it is dry?"

ARGUMENT AGAINST AUTHENTICITY

These verses are a Christian prophecy that Luke has put into the mouth of Jesus when on his way to the cross. It further reinforces the anti-Judaism of Luke's passion narrative. The lamentation should not be for Jesus but for the inhabitants of Jerusalem, whose harsh punishment will be the destruction of their city in 70 CE. (As does Matthew in the previous passage, Luke here plays the Monday-morning quarterback). The lamenting women represent the Jewish people, who are in turn represented by the witnesses to the crucifixion (Luke 23:35, 48). Verse 29, which echoes Luke 21:23, is a paraphrase of Isa 54:1; it recalls Luke 11:27, in which a supportive female in an otherwise antagonistic Jewish crowd cries out, "Blessed is the womb that bore you and the breasts you sucked." Here, of course, a contrary sentiment is assigned to the women of Jerusalem. Verse 30 then cites the doom pronounced in Hos 10:8, and verse 31 offers what may be a somewhat cryptic allusion to Prov 11:31 by way of explaining the punishment to befall Jerusalem. The words come from Luke, not Jesus.

18

End of the World and Judgment

Mark 13:5b–13

The beginning of the birth pangs

5b"Look out that no one LEADS you ASTRAY. 6Many will come in my name and say, 'I am he,' and will LEAD many ASTRAY.

7"And when you hear of wars and the tumult of war, do not be afraid. It must happen thus. But the end is not yet. 8For nation will rise up against nation, and kingdom against kingdom. Some places will endure earthquakes, and some will suffer famines. That is the beginning of the birth pangs.

9 "But be on the lookout. They will *hand* you *over* to the courts, and in the synagogues you will be scourged, and you will be led before governors and kings for my sake, as a testimony to them.

10"And first the gospel must be preached to all nations.

11"And when they lead you away and *hand* you *over*, do not be anxious in advance about what you should say; but say whatever is given to you in that hour. For it is not you that speak, but the Holy Spirit.

12"And brother will *hand over* his brother to death and the father his child, and children will rage against parents and will kill them.

13"And you will be hated by all for my name's sake. But that person who perseveres to the end, will be saved."

ARGUMENT AGAINST AUTHENTICITY

Verses 5–8 contain a summary survey in which verse 6 anticipates verses 21–22 (see below, p. 57). It should also be noted that at the outset Mark turns to the teaching about Christ. Many will falsely claim to be the Jesus who has returned and speak in his name. However, the events described in verses 7 and 8 are only the beginning.

These purported sayings of Jesus derive from a series of crises that beset the early Christian communities years after his death. As 2 John 7 shows, eschatological adversaries were expected in the Johannine community, and Christian teachers with different leanings were considered to be a danger by many a Christian community. In order to defend themselves against those they considered heretics, community leaders claimed that Jesus had already predicted the coming of these false teachers. Clearly, it did not take long to discover and fill the need for a saying of Jesus that attacked those who spread contrary doctrines.

In the next section, verses 9–13, the imperative "look out" corresponds to that in verse 5 (cf. verse 23). The section reflects the experiences of Mark's community, whose present situation and aspiration is described in verse 10. The mission to the Gentiles was in full swing and—of course—backed up by a saying of Jesus. Furthermore, the delay in the return of Jesus is seen as part of God's plan. The "Holy Spirit" (verse 11) is a phenomenon of the post-Easter period, as are the family and societal schisms mentioned in verses 12 and 13. The extreme language no doubt echoes Micah 7:6 ("The son treats the father with contempt, the daughter rises up against her mother, the daughter-in-law against her mother-in-law; a man's enemies are the men of his own house") and reflects a crisis situation. Hatred occasioned by the name of Jesus belongs to a later time, when Christianity flourished and Christian Jews distinguished themselves from other Jewish communities.

Mark 13:14–23

The turning point of history

[14]"But when you see 'the abomination of desolation' [Dan 11:31; 12:11] standing where it should not—let the reader note—then those in Judea should flee to the mountains. [15]The one on the

roof should not descend and go in to get something from his house. [16]And the one in the field should not turn back to get his coat. [17]And woe to the pregnant and those who are breast-feeding in those days.

[18]"Pray that it does not happen in winter. [19]For those days will be a tribulation such as has never been from the beginning of God's creation until now, nor will there be again (cf. Dan 12:1]. [20]And had the Lord not *cut short those days*, no one would be saved. But for the sake of the *elect*, whom he has chosen, he has *cut short those days*.

[21]"If then anyone says to you, 'Look, here is the Christ!' or 'Look, there he is!' do not believe it. [22]For false Christs and false prophets will appear, and they will do signs and wonders to attempt to lead astray the *elect*.

[23]"But be on the lookout! I have told you all this in advance."

ARGUMENT AGAINST AUTHENTICITY

Verses 14–20 depict the transition from the Markan community's present to its future. Verse 14 represents a key to the understanding not only of this discourse, but also to the Gospel of Mark generally. Both verse 14a and verse 19 are stamped with clear reference to the book of Daniel. "Jesus" invites the readers to understand the forthcoming events against the background of the experience and thought of the prophet Daniel, i.e. to understand the decree erecting of the statue of the emperor in the Jerusalem temple specifically in terms of the "abomination of desolation" in the book of Daniel. For this action marks the beginning of the tribulation that signifies the end time. Verses 21–22 correspond to a Q saying (Matt 24:26–27/Luke 17:23–24). They connect the passage with the topic of teachings about Christ presented at the outset in Mark 13:6 (see above, p. 55). The segment ends in verse 23 with a renewed appeal ("Be on the lookout!") and with reference to Jesus, who has predicted everything and whose words therefore cannot be canceled or modified by later events. Inasmuch as "Jesus" knew everything in advance (cf. Mark 11:2–6) and handed on his knowledge to the community, the community need not be worried.

Obviously, all this is the voice of the early church, not that of the historical Jesus.

Mark 13:24–27

The turning point of salvation history: the coming of the Son of man.

24"But in those days, after that affliction,

> the sun will be darkened,
> and the moon will not give its light; [Isa 13:10]
> 25and the stars will fall from the sky,
> and the heavenly bodies will be shaken. [Isa 34:4]

26At that time they will see 'the Son of man coming in clouds' [Dan 7:13] with great power and glory. 27And then he will send his angels and will bring together his elect from the four winds, from the end of the earth to the end of heaven."

ARGUMENT AGAINST AUTHENTICITY

This section contains speculations about the end of the world. The authors of these verses are the "elect" who hoped to be gathered into eternal life by the Son of man, Jesus, during their lifetimes. Note that in the three predictions of the suffering and resurrection in the Gospel of Mark, "Jesus" spoke about the Son of man in the third person but meant himself (see above, pp. 15–17).

Matthew 25:31–46

The judgment of the world

31"When the Son of man comes in his glory, and all the angels with him, he will sit on the throne of his glory, 32and all the peoples will be gathered before him. And he will separate them one from another as a shepherd separates the sheep from the goats,

³³and he will place the sheep at his right hand, but the goats at the left.

³⁴**"Then the king will say to those on his right hand, 'Come, you blessed of my Father; inherit the kingdom prepared for you from the foundation of the world.**

³⁵*"'For I was hungry and you gave me to eat, I was thirsty and you gave me to drink, I was a stranger and you welcomed me,* ³⁶*I was naked and you clothed me. I was sick and you visited me. I was in prison and you came to me.'*

³⁷"THEN THE RIGHTEOUS WILL ANSWER HIM, 'LORD, WHEN DID WE SEE YOU HUNGRY AND GIVE YOU TO EAT, OR THIRSTY AND GIVE YOU TO DRINK? ³⁸WHEN DID WE SEE YOU A STRANGER AND INVITE YOU IN, OR NAKED AND CLOTHE YOU? ³⁹WHEN DID WE SEE YOU SICK OR IN PRISON AND VISIT YOU?'

⁴⁰"And the king will answer, 'Truly, I SAY TO YOU, WHATEVER YOU DID FOR ONE OF THE LEAST OF THESE BROTHERS OF MINE, YOU DID FOR ME.'

⁴¹**"Then he will say to those at his left hand, 'Depart from me, you cursed, into the eternal fire prepared for the devil and his angels.**

⁴²*"'For I was hungry and you gave me nothing to eat, I was thirsty and you gave me nothing to drink,* ⁴³*I was a stranger and you did not welcome me, I was naked and you did not clothe me, I was sick and in prison and you did not visit me.'*

⁴⁴"THEN THEY ALSO WILL ANSWER HIM, 'LORD, WHEN DID WE SEE YOU HUNGRY OR THIRSTY OR A STRANGER OR NEEDING CLOTHES OR SICK OR IN PRISON, AND DID NOT MINISTER TO YOU?'

⁴⁵"Then he will answer them, 'TRULY, I SAY TO YOU, WHAT YOU HAVE NOT DONE TO ONE OF THE LEAST OF THESE, YOU HAVE NOT DONE FOR ME.'

⁴⁶**"And these will go away into eternal punishment, but the righteous into eternal life."**

ARGUMENT AGAINST AUTHENTICITY

In this section, which is often wrongly headed "*Parable* of the judgment of the world," we find two powerful dialogues (verses 34–40 and verses 41–45) with a strikingly symmetrical construction. The moral of the passage corresponds to Isa 58:7: "Break your bread with the hungry and bring the homeless poor into your house. When you see the naked, clothe him" (cf. also Ezek 18:7, 16).

This concluding text of Jesus' eschatological discourse is quite naturally in perfect accord with Matthew's theology. After the exhortation in Matt 24:32–25:30, the judgment of the Son of man is depicted in panoramic fashion. The judgment includes all human beings, but Matthew shines a spotlight on his particular community: see especially Matt 13:37–43, 49–50. Verse 40 (cf. verse 45) completes the identification of the Son of man with the least of these brothers (see Matt 10:42; 18:6, 10, 14). In view of the clear similarities, we have considerable justification for concluding that Matthew fabricated the whole passage.

19

Rules of Piety

Matthew 6:1–6, 16–18
About almsgiving, prayer, and fasting

[1]"Beware of practicing your righteousness before people in order to be noticed by them; for then you will have no reward from your Father who is in heaven."

[2] "So WHEN YOU give *alms*, you are not to sound a trumpet before you, as the *HYPOCRITES* do in the synagogues and in the streets, that they may by praised by people. *TRULY, I SAY TO YOU, THEY ALREADY HAVE THEIR REWARD.* [3]Instead, when giving *alms*, do not let your left hand know what your right hand is doing, [4]so that your *alms* may be *IN SECRET*.

"AND YOUR FATHER WHO SEES *IN SECRET* WILL RECOMPENSE YOU."

[5]"And WHEN YOU **pray**, do not be like the *HYPOCRITES*, for they love to stand and **pray** in the synagogues and on the street corners to PUT THEMSELVES ON SHOW to people. *TRULY, I SAY TO YOU, THEY ALREADY HAVE THEIR REWARD.* [6]Instead, WHEN YOU **pray**, go into your room, close the door and **pray** to your Father, who is *IN SECRET*.

"AND YOUR FATHER WHO SEES *IN SECRET* WILL RECOMPENSE YOU. . . ."

[16]"And WHEN YOU *fast*, do not look dismal like the *HYPOCRITES*, for they disfigure their faces so as to PUT THEMSELVES ON SHOW to people as *fasting*. *I ASSURE YOU THAT THEY ALREADY HAVE THEIR REWARD.* [17]Instead, when *fasting*, anoint your head and wash your face [18]so as not to PUT YOURSELF ON SHOW to people as *fasting* but only to your Father who is *IN SECRET*.

"AND YOUR FATHER WHO SEES *IN SECRET* WILL RECOMPENSE YOU."

ARGUMENT AGAINST AUTHENTICITY

Three rules about piety form the core of this section. Their construction is symmetrical and each time they are introduced by a "when" clause (verses 2, 5, 16). They deal with almsgiving (verses 2–4), prayer (verses 5–6) and fasting (verses 16–18). Note that Matthew has composed and inserted the so-called Lord's Prayer (verses 9–13) preceded by an introduction (verses 7–8) into the existing tradition as an example of an appropriately brief prayer, and added a homiletic comment (verses 14–15), neither of which I shall discuss here.

The rules of piety have a structure deriving from wisdom. Since they concentrate on inward behavior, public worship in the temple is not mentioned; the individual stands at the center. Radical asceticism is called for as a personal attitude.

Matthew has headed the entire section with the introductory verse 1, linguistic elements of which suggest its editorial origin: note in particular the designation of God as "Father in heaven" and the term "righteousness". Clearly, the First Evangelist has deliberately categorized the subsequent three rules of piety, which comprised a traditional catechism, under the theme of righteousness.

Jesus did not speak these words. *First*, they have nothing to do with his call to repentance, which is grounded in the imminence of the kingdom of God and his radical ethical demands. *Second*, the rules about fasting stand in direct opposition to the authentic saying of Jesus in Mark 2:19, according to which the presence of the bridegroom Jesus makes the observance of the commandment about fasting superfluous. By contrast, Mark 2:20, which describes the time after the death and "resurrection" of Jesus, states, "The days will come when the bridegroom is taken away from them, and then they will fast in that day."

This is the situation in which rules about fasting like those in Matt 6:16–18 could have been developed. But if these are inauthentic, then the formal correspondence of the sayings indicates that the same is also to be said of the first and second rules. *Third*, although Jesus' reported condemnation of these same three forms of piety in Thomas 14:1–3 is doubtless inauthentic, its very existence shows the polemical nature of these issues in the early church, and thus casts further doubt on the notion that Jesus had given specific directions on these matters.

20

Catalogue of Vices

Mark 7:20b–23

What defiles a person

20b"It is what comes out of a person, that **defiles** the person.
21aFor from within, from the human heart, come evil thoughts,
    21bfornications, thefts, murders,
    22adulteries, covetousnesses, wickednesses,
    deceit, licentiousness, the evil eye,
    blasphemy, arrogance, failure to understand.
23All these evils come from within and **defile** the person."

ARGUMENT AGAINST AUTHENTICITY

Mark misunderstands the foregoing dispute (Mark 7:1–5) about what is clean and unclean: he sees it from the perspective of behavior rather than that of purity regulations (cf. similarly the insertion of Mark 7:6–8 and 7:9–13). Formally speaking, verses 21b–22 are a catalogue of vices, and they come from Mark's community or from the writer himself. The individual sins are literarily arranged in two groups of three, once in the plural and then in the singular, and constitute an antithetical definition of the Christian life.

Other examples of catalogues of vices can be found in several of the New Testament letters, but they are oriented on Greek philosophical ethics. See Rom 1:29–31; 1 Cor 5:10; 6:9–10; 2 Cor 12:20; Gal 5:19–21; 1 Pet 4:3. The several Jesus traditions contain but one catalogue of vices, Mark 7:21b–21. It is surely not authentic.

21

Consolation for Christians under Persecution

Matthew 5:11

Blessing of persecuted Christians

[11]"Blessed are you when they revile you and persecute you and utter all kinds of evil against you falsely for my sake."

ARGUMENT AGAINST AUTHENTICITY

The oldest beatitudes—those that promise a swift reversal of their situation to people who are poor, who are hungry, and who are weeping—go back to the historical Jesus (cf. Luke 6:20–21). Note that these authentic beatitudes are not self-referring. The situation changes in the post-Easter community, for now Jesus is part of the beatitude with followers being included, as we see in Matt 5:11 and in the parallel Luke 6:22. These beatitudes tell of followers being punished for being his disciples—no case of which is reported to have happened during his lifetime—and therefore must reflect the negative experiences of Christians in the hostile environment that developed much later.

Matthew 10:17–22

Persevering until the end

[17]"Beware of people; for they will **hand** you **over** to courts and they will flog you in their synagogues. [18]And for my sake you will be led before governors and kings, to bear witness to them and the Gentiles.

[19]"But when they **hand** you **over**, do not worry about what to *say* or how to *say* it. For at that hour it will be given to you what you should *say*. [20]For it is not you *who speak*, but the Spirit of your Father is the one *who speaks* in you.

[21]"And a brother will **hand over** (his) brother to death, and the father (the) child; and the children will rise against parents and will kill them.

65

²²All you will be hated by all for my name's sake.
But whoever perseveres to the end will be saved."

ARGUMENT AGAINST AUTHENTICITY

Matthew has taken this section from Mark 13:9–13 (see above. pp. 55–56) where it describes the daily experience of following Jesus. By transferring it to the context of sending forth the disciples, Matthew sheds light on the fate of the missionaries.

Verses 17–20 are words of encouragement spoken by community leaders to missionaries, promising the sanction and protection of Jesus' name. Verses 21–22 reflect experiences of Christian communities.

Matthew 10:28–33

Invitation to fearless confession

²⁸ "*Do not fear* those who kill the body but cannot kill the soul.
Fear rather the one who can destroy both soul and body in hell.

²⁹Are not two **sparrows** bought for a penny?
Yet not one of them falls to the ground without your Father.
³⁰Even all the hairs of your head are numbered.
³¹So *do not fear*, you are worth more than many **sparrows**.

³²Therefore, everyone who CONFESSES ME
   BEFORE THE PEOPLE,
I will also CONFESS
   BEFORE MY FATHER IN THE HEAVENS.
³³But whoever *DENIES* ME
   BEFORE THE PEOPLE,
I will also *DENY*
   BEFORE MY FATHER IN THE HEAVENS "

ARGUMENT AGAINST AUTHENTICITY

This section is held together by the commandment not to fear any but God. Verses 28–31 constitute a comforting assurance of personal worth, and thereby indicate that the main concern here is the threat of persecution. Verse 32 makes explicit the promise of divine favor for those who suffer for Jesus' sake, and verses 32–33 taken together recall Matt 7:21–23 and 25:34: the faithful will be rewarded, but even a disciple may be damned if he or she is reprobate. Not only does this repeated leitmotiv suggest the presence of an authorial hand, but the combination of promise and threat fits best in a post-Easter situation.

All the sayings in this section derive from a later situation in which the community is attempting to deal with persecution.

John 15:18–16:15
The hatred of the world and the
coming of the Paraclete

[1] ¹⁸**"If** the WORLD HATES you,
know that it has HATED me before (it hated) you.
¹⁹If you were of the WORLD, the WORLD would love its own. Yet because you are not of the WORLD, but I have chosen you out of the WORLD, therefore the WORLD HATES you. ^{20a}Remember the word that I said to you: 'The slave is not greater than his lord.' [John 13:16]

[2] ^{20b}**If** they persecuted me,
they will also persecute you.

[3] ^{20c}**If** they have observed my word,
they will observe yours also.
²¹But all this they will do to you for my name's sake, for they do not know him who has sent me.

[4] ²²**If** I had not come and spoken to them, *they would not have sin.*
But now they have no excuse for their sin.
²³He who HATES me, HATES my FATHER also.

[5] ²⁴**If** I had not done among them the works that no one else did, *they would not have sin.*
But now they have seen (them) and nevertheless HATE both me and my FATHER.

²⁵But it is to fulfill the word that is written in their law, 'They HATED me without a cause.'" [Ps 35:19; 69:5]

²⁶"But when the **PARACLETE** comes, whom I will send to you from the FATHER, the Spirit of truth who proceeds from the FATHER, he will bear witness to me. ²⁷And you will also bear witness, because you have been with me FROM THE BEGINNING.

16:1 "I have spoken this (to) you so that you will not fall away.

² "They will exclude you from the synagogue; and even now, the *HOUR* is coming when whoever kills you will think he is offering a service to God. ³And they will do this because they have not known the FATHER nor me. ⁴But I have spoken these things to you so that when their *HOUR* comes, you may remember that I have told you of them.

"I did not say this to you FROM THE BEGINNING, because I was with you.

⁵"But now I am going to him who sent me, and none of you asks me, 'Where are you going?' ⁶But because I have said these things to you, sorrow has filled your hearts. ⁷Yet I tell you the truth: it is to your advantage that I go away. For if I do not go away, the **PARACLETE** will not come to you. But if I depart, I will send him to you.

⁸"And when he comes, he will convict the *WORLD* of its error
regarding sin,
and regarding righteousness,
and regarding judgment:

⁹regarding sin,
because they do not believe in me;
¹⁰regarding righteousness,
because I go to the FATHER and you will see me no
more;
¹¹regarding judgment,
because the ruler of this *WORLD* has been judged.

¹²I have yet many things to say to you, but you cannot bear them now. ¹³But when he comes, the **SPIRIT OF TRUTH**, he will guide you into all the truth. For he will not speak of his own accord; but

whatever he hears, he will speak,
and *he will disclose to you* the things that are to come.
¹⁴He will glorify me, for
HE WILL TAKE OF WHAT IS MINE
and *disclose it to you*.
¹⁵All that the FATHER has is mine; therefore I said that
HE TAKES OF WHAT IS MINE
and *will disclose it to you*."

ARGUMENT AGAINST AUTHENTICITY

This section belongs to John 15–17, the farewell discourses, which like John 21 are separate units within the Fourth Gospel. Since in this book I examine a number of passages from John 15–17, I here offer a brief introduction to demonstrate that these chapters were later additions the Fourth Gospel.

First, John 18:1 is the organic continuation of the signal to depart in John 14:31c ("Arise, let us go from here!"); see also the analogous transition from Mark 14:42 to Mark 14:43. *Second*, the transition from 14:31 to 15:1 is particularly harsh. *Third*, the farewell discourse in John 13:31–14:31 represents a coherent and self-contained whole: in it Jesus has said all that the disciples need to know. Moreover the impression that any further word would be superfluous is reinforced by John 14:30a: having there made the announcement "I will no longer talk much with you", it seems strange that Jesus would immediately commence a new discourse—and, for that matter, the longest to appear in the Gospel. *Fourth*, the discourses in chapters 15–17 hang in the air without any apparent setting until in John 18:1 the somewhat absurd situation arises that they were spoken upon departure of Jesus and the disciples from the place of their final supper to the garden beyond the brook Kidron. *Fifth*, chapters 15–17 show numerous deviations and shifts of accent from the theological tendency of the rest of the Gospel.

However, chapters 15–17 were not introduced into the Gospel all at once. Rather, there are several indications that the individual sections contained in them, namely John 15:1–17; 15:18–16:15; 16:16–33; and 17:1–26, were added in stages by different authors. For one thing, these sections display differences not only from the Gospel but also from one another. Besides, they are unified and well-rounded in themselves. And finally, the repeated occurrences of particular concluding phrases (e.g. "I have spoken this to you"; "I have yet many things to say to you, but . . .") indicate that different authors are writing endings for individual sections.

The theme of the section currently under analysis, John 15:18–16:15—namely, the hatred of this world towards the community and the coming of the Paraclete—has nothing to do with that of the preceding discourse (John 15:1–17), which is the admonition to abide in Christ and to love one another. This fact alone suggests that different authors are speaking, and that inference is reinforced by the fact that John 15:20a refers to John 13:16 in a different way from John 15:15. Whereas according to John 15:15 Jesus will no longer call the disciples slaves, in John 15:20 he derives the world's enmity towards the disciples from the fact that these are "slaves" and as such must suffer the same fate as their Lord.

The basis of this section seems to be a revelation discourse that consists of five "if-sentences" (John 15:18, 20b, 20c, 22, 24). In a threefold variation it describes the union between Jesus and his community and afterwards renders judgment against the sinful behavior of the world. Inasmuch as it presupposes a community that is stamped by failure and hostility, none of the five elements can possibly derive from the historical Jesus. That is especially true with respect to the extensive additions (John 15:26–16:15) that focus on the actions and role of the Paraclete, a figure whom the Jesus of the first three New Testament Gospels never mentions.

Verses 26–27: The promise of the support of the Comforter or Holy Spirit occurs also in the Synoptic traditions about persecutions (cf. Mark 13:11–13; Matt 10:19–20; Luke 12:11–12). However, in contrast to the Fourth Evangelist (see John 14:16–17, 26) the Synoptic authors do not identify the Paraclete with the Exalted One, whereas John envisions an independent entity who is sent by Jesus himself and not by the Father (cf. John 16:7).

Verse 16:1: This verse sums up the remarks so far and indicates their purpose, which is to immunize the disciples against apostasy.

Verses 4b–7: For the first time since John 13:31–14:31, Jesus explicitly mentions the imminence of his farewell. In view of the sorrow with which the disciples are stricken by the announcement in John 15:18–25, Jesus now speaks of the benefit of his going away, namely, the coming of the Paraclete (cf. John 15:26–27). In verse 5 the present author creates a contradiction with the farewell discourse composed by the Evangelist. In that framework (see John 13:36) the question "Where are you going?" was certainly addressed to Jesus.

Verses 8–11: These verses deal with the Paraclete's task of judging and convicting a sinful world. This is first described summarily in verse 8 and then developed in a threefold pattern in verses 9–11. The sense of the remarks, which are compressed and therefore difficult to understand, is probably as follows: The Paraclete will convict the world of its sin, because it is hostile to Jesus as the Revealer sent by God (verse 9); he will disclose the righteousness of Jesus, whose exaltation will be revealed (verse 10); and finally he will show that the violent death of Jesus is in truth the defeat of the ruler of this world (verse 11; cf. John 12:31, 16:33).

Verse 12: This verse introduces the end of the present addition.

Verses 13–15: Verses 13–14 deal with the activity of the Paraclete in the community. After Jesus' departure the Paraclete will make up for what Jesus can no longer say to his disciples now because they could not bear it in the sorrowful situation of the farewell (verse 12). Again, note that this does not correspond to what "Jesus" had said earlier about the Paraclete, namely, that his function was merely to remind the disciples of what "Jesus" has already revealed completely and finally (cf. John 14:26). Verse 15, which quotes the verse directly preceding it, might well be seen as an emphatic or clarifying pleonasm. The formulation "all that the Father has is mine" suggests that it derives from the author of chapter 17 (cf. John 17:10).

John 16:16–33
Sorrow and joy; Speaking in riddles and speaking openly

¹⁶"A LITTLE WHILE, AND YOU DO NOT SEE ME anymore, AND AGAIN A LITTLE WHILE, AND YOU WILL SEE ME."

¹⁷Then (some) of his disciples said to one another, "What is this that he says to us, 'A LITTLE WHILE, AND YOU DO NOT SEE ME, AND AGAIN A LITTLE WHILE, AND YOU WILL SEE ME'; and, 'I go to the Father'?"

¹⁸ Now they said, "What is this, 'a little while'? We do not know what he is talking about."

¹⁹Jesus knew that they wanted to ask him, and said to them, "Are you discussing among yourselves what I meant when I said, 'A LITTLE WHILE, AND YOU WILL NOT SEE ME, AND AGAIN A LITTLE WHILE, AND YOU WILL SEE ME?'

²⁰ *"Truly, truly, I say to you,*
    you will weep and lament,
        but the *WORLD* will *REJOICE.*
    You will be in PAIN,
        but your PAIN will turn to *JOY.*

²¹A woman, when she is giving birth, has PAIN because her **HOUR** has come; but when she has given birth to the child she

no longer remembers the hurt because of her *JOY* that a human being has come into the WORLD.

²²"So you too have PAIN now, but I will see you again and your hearts will *REJOICE*, and no one will take your *JOY* from you. ²³And on that day you will ask nothing of me.

"*Truly, truly, I say to you*, if you ask anything of the FATHER, he will give it to you *in my name*. ²⁴Up to now you have not asked for anything *in my name*. Ask, and you will receive, that your *JOY* may be complete.

²⁵"I have said this to you in **RIDDLES**; yet the **HOUR** is coming when I will no longer speak to you in **RIDDLES**, but tell you openly of the FATHER. ²⁶On that day you will ask *in my name*; and I do not say that I will pray to the FATHER on your behalf, ²⁷for the FATHER himself loves you because you have come to love me and **have come to believe** that *I came forth from the* FATHER.

²⁸ *I came forth from the* FATHER
>> and have come into the WORLD;
>> again, I leave the WORLD
and go to the FATHER."

²⁹His disciples reply, "Look, now you are speaking plainly, and not in **RIDDLES**. ³⁰Now we can see that you know all things and that you do not even need to have anyone ask you questions; therefore we **believe** that *you have come forth from God.*"

³¹Jesus answered them, "Do you now **believe**? ³²ᵃLook, the **HOUR** is coming, and in fact already has, when you will be scattered, every one to his own home, and will leave me alone. ³²ᵇYet I am not alone, for the FATHER is with me.

³³ᵃ"I have spoken this to you so that in me you may have peace. ³³ᵇIn the WORLD you have affliction; but be consoled! I have conquered the WORLD."

ARGUMENT AGAINST AUTHENTICITY

The author of this third addition (cf. the introduction to chapters 15–17 above, pp. 69–70) is not identical with the author of John 15:18–16:15. This emerges above all from the fact that in contrast to the previous writer he does not refer to the Paraclete. As numerous parallel formulations and allusions show, the author of John 16:16–33 has especially modeled his work on the farewell discourse John 13:31–14:31, while also employing echoes from other parts of the Gospel (cf. the references in the following analysis). So in literary terms this section is dependent on its context and was especially composed to fit into it smoothly.

Verse 16: Jesus announces to his disciples the immediate separation and promises them that they will see him again soon (cf. John 14:19; see also 7:33; 13:33). Here the first span of time is meant to be the time from the situation imagined for the discourse to the death of Jesus, and the second is the time from Jesus' death to Easter. There can be no doubt that Easter—and not the parousia—is intended, for the prayer of supplication to which Jesus invites the disciples in verses 23–24 would be superfluous after his return. Furthermore, it cannot be a coincidence that several phrases and terms that appear in John 16:16–33 will be found again in connection with the Easter narratives: cf. "on that day" (John 16:23, 26 and 20:19 with 14:20); "joy" (John 16:20, 22, 24 and 20:20); "peace" (John 16:33 and 20:19, 21); and "see" (John 16:16, 17, 19, 22, and John 20:20).

Verses 17–18: For the first time since John 13:31–14:31 the disciples again play a role. Here, however, they do not appear as individuals (cf. John 14:5, 8, 22), but as a group. They express their incomprehension about the announcement in verse 16. According to verse 17 they also ask about the meaning of the saying "I go to the Father". This is strange, since Jesus did not say any such thing in verse 16. But this saying does appear in John 16:10 (cf. previously John 13:3, 33, 36; 14:4–5, 28; 16:5). Evidently this is a literary hook for the author of John 16:16–33 to fix his own addition in the context of the farewell discourses.

Verse 19: By virtue of his capacity to see into people's minds and hearts, Jesus knows the thoughts of his disciples (for this motif, which is also often used by the Evangelist, cf. John 1:42).

Verses 20–22: These verses are governed by the key words "pain" and "joy". Here verses 20 and 22 correspond in content: the time of the seeing-no-longer will be a painful time, and that of the seeing-again at Easter a joyful one. Verse 21 illustrates the transition from one to the other with the help of an image common in the Old Testament (cf. Isa 66:7–10; see also Isa 21:3; 26:17–18; 37:3).

The statement "no one takes your joy from you" shows that by "Easter" the author evidently does not merely understand the short space of time in which the Risen One will dwell visibly and physically among the disciples, but the post-Easter period generally.

Verses 23–24: With "Easter," which in this awareness continues to recur, the questions of the disciples come to an end (verse 23a) because they will then have direct access to God (verses 23b–24). God himself will hear their prayers (cf. John 15:7, 16; but according to John 14:13 the exalted Jesus will hear the prayers of the disciples.) For "complete joy" cf. John 15:11.

Verse 25: This verse introduces the second part of the addition, in which the theme is the opposition between riddle and open talk.

Verses 26–27: The promise that prayer will be heard corresponds to verses 23–24. The saying about the Father's love refers to John 14:21b, 23a.

Verse 28: For the formulation cf. John 13:3b.

Verses 29–30: The disciples think that they already possess what, according to verse 25, Jesus had promised them only for the time after Easter. Here verse 30a in part points back to 2:25.

Verses 31–32: Because the disciples presume to understand now, whereas complete understanding can come only with the Easter experiences, Jesus rebukes them (for the question in verse 31 cf. John 1:50; 20:29; see also John 13:38). By predicting that they will desert him in his passion, he shows them the premature and indeed questionable nature of the certainty of faith that they have expressed. This evidently alludes to the tradition of the flight of the disciples found in Mark 14:27, 50/Matt 26:31, 56. Verse 32b corresponds to John 8:16b and possibly represents an indirect criticism of Mark 15:34.

Verse 33a: With its promise of peace (cf. John 14:27), this verse introduces the end of the discourse.

Verse 33b: This verse recalls Jesus' statement about his superiority to the ruler of the world in John 14:30 (cf. 12:31). Unlike the latter passage, however, this one shows him speaking from the standpoint of the exalted Christ: despite the crucifixion of the Son of God, the world has not been able challenge Jesus' union with the Father. That is its defeat and Jesus' victory.

Along with John 15:18–16:15, this section belongs to the farewell discourses which, according to the Fourth Gospel, Jesus addresses to his disciples on the eve of his death. They are permeated by the conviction that on the evening of the day of resurrection (John 20:19–23) Jesus will see his disciples again. Clearly, therefore, these speeches are later theological reflections retroactively attributed to Jesus.

22

Community Discipline and Leaders' Authority

Matthew 16:18b–19

Peter named the church's foundation

[18b]"You are Peter ('the rock'), and on this rock I will build my church, and the gates of hell shall not prevail against it.

[19] "I will give you the keys of the kingdom of the heavens,
  and whatever you shall bind on earth
    shall be bound in the heavens,
  and whatever you loose on earth
    shall be loosed in the heavens."

ARGUMENT AGAINST AUTHENTICITY

Matthew has inserted the present passage into Mark's text (Mark 8:27–30), which he had in front of him. The beatitude of Peter is Jesus' response to Peter's confession that Jesus is the Christ, the son of the living God (cf. Mark 8:29).

This addition gives Peter decisive authority over discipline and teaching, a commission inherent in the verbs "bind" and "loose" in verse 19. Jesus cannot have spoken these words because he did not found a church. Rather, this is a saying of the "Risen Christ" deriving from the report (1 Cor 15:5) that Cephas (the Aramaic equivalent of the Greek *Petros*, Peter) was the first witness to the resurrection of Jesus, i.e. he was the first to see Jesus in heavenly glory. These words were then assigned to Jesus either by Peter himself or his followers, and subsequently added by Matthew to his account of Jesus' life.

Matthew 18:15–20

Rules of the community

[15]"If **your brother** sins against you,
  show him his fault while you are alone with him.

If he **listens** to you,
> you have gained **your brother**.

[16]But if he does not *listen*,
> take one or TWO other members along, so that

>> every matter may be established
>> by the testimony of TWO or three witnesses. [Deut 19:15]

[17]But if he does not to *listen* to them,
> take the issue to the community;
and if he does not to *listen* even to the community,
> let him be to you as a Gentile or a tax collector.
[18]Truly, truly, I say to you,
whatever you bind ON EARTH
> will be bound *in heaven*,
and whatever you loose ON EARTH
> will be loosed *in heaven*.
[19]Again, I say to you, whenever TWO of you agree ON EARTH
about anything they ask, it will be granted to them by my Father
in the heavens.

> [20]"For where TWO *or three* come together in my name, I am in
their midst."

ARGUMENT AGAINST AUTHENTICITY

The section consists of two parts, verses 15–18 and verses 19–20.

Verses 15–17 place on the lips of Jesus a disciplinary or-der for the Matthean community, giving procedural rules for dealing with a situation when one member has committed a sin against another. If no reconciliation is achieved, the accused brother is to be ostracized. It is noteworthy that here the community is still living completely apart from the Gentiles (see also Matt 6:7). Verse 18 was added to verses 15–17 at a secondary stage, as its content has nothing to do with community discipline, but rather serves as an en-dorsement to the procedure in verses 15–17. According to

"Jesus," God will confirm the community's verdict on the unrepentant sinner (cf. Matt 16:19).

Contrary to appearances, verses 19–20 have a close connection with verses 15–17 (see the links indicated by italics). Matthew also connects this passage with verse 18 by its introductory word, "again," and intends it to authenticate the power of the community's prayer, especially inasmuch as it represents their coming together in the name of Jesus (verse 20).

The historical value of the passage under discussion is nil: Verses 15–17 are completely rooted in a particular community situation after the death of Jesus, and for that reason alone cannot go back to him. The same is true of verse 18, which as a saying of Jesus gives the community heavenly sanctions for its effective jurisdiction. And since verses 19–20 derive from the Easter situation (cf. Matt 28:20), the heavenly Savior is speaking, not the historical Jesus.

23

Sending the Disciples to all Nations

Matthew 28:18b–20
Mission charge

[18b]"I was given all authority in heaven and on earth.

[19]"Therefore go and make disciples of all nations [the Gentiles], baptizing them in the name of the Father and of the Son and of the Holy Spirit, [20]and teaching them to observe all that I have commanded you.

"And look, I am with you always, to the end of time."

ARGUMENT AGAINST AUTHENTICITY

Quite apart from the fact that the "Risen Christ" is speaking in this text, the words attributed to Jesus are wholly rooted in the situation of a community which, after his death, is actively engaged in a Gentile mission and no longer addresses the gospel to fellow Jews. With its mission command, verse 19 deliberately points back to Matt 10:5–6. Its target is exclusively Gentile, for "nations" must be understood in the same way as in Matt 10:5–6 and here, namely as non-Jews. Matthew would hardly have counted the Jews among the nations. Obviously, this rejection of Jewish converts had not always been the case, as we see in Matt 10:5–6, where the disciples are sent exclusively to "the lost sheep of Israel."

This text presupposes a situation corresponding to that described in Matthew 21:33–23:39, where the Gentile church has taken the place of Israel. According to this supersessionist theory, unbelieving Israel is damned to hell because of its guilt for the killing of Jesus and his messengers.

The parable of the Wicked Tenants (Mark 12:1b–11: see above, pp. 37–38), which Matthew had in front of him, had likewise indicated that the Jewish people had been deprived of its preferential status and that the "vineyard," i.e. the

Chosen People's special place in salvation history, would be given to others (Mark 12:9). Matthew developed this idea even more consistently: the "other tenants" will deliver the fruits of the vineyard to the owner—in contrast to the Jewish people, who brought forth no fruit (Matt 21:41). This corresponds to the threatening pronouncement directed to the chief priests and the Pharisees: ". . . the kingdom of God will be taken away from you and given to a people that produces the fruits of the kingdom" (Matt 21:43). Israel loses its position of pre-eminence as it loses its participation in the kingdom of God. Note that Matt 21:43 is expressed in the future tense; it does not deal with the eschatological future but with the historical future, and thus describes something that had already happened in the time of Jesus. The kingdom of God has been taken away from the Jews and transferred to another people, the church.

To be sure, Matthew presents the Jewish people as at first an approving chorus that responds to Jesus' mighty deeds with applause, admiration, amazement, and shock. But it is characteristic of Matthew's point of view that at the end of Jesus' life "the whole people" join with the chief priests and elders in demanding the death of Jesus (Matt 27:20), and accepting the terrible consequence: "His blood be on us and our children!" (Matt 27:25). Matthew intentionally emphasizes that the Jewish people as a whole is involved in the cry for Jesus' crucifixion and invokes on itself the destruction of Jerusalem that was to happen in the near future as its punishment (Matt 24:2). Israel's special standing before God comes to an end with the crucifixion of Jesus, and the kingdom of God is given to another people.

24

Parables on Various Topics

Luke 16:19–31

Rich man and poor Lazarus

¹⁹There was a RICH man who clothed himself in purple and finest linen and feasted sumptuously every day.

²⁰And at his gate lay a POOR man named *LAZARUS*, covered with *sores* ²¹and longing to be filled with what fell from the RICH man's table. And even the dogs came and licked his *sores*.

²²Now it happened that the POOR man died and was carried by angels to ABRAHAM's *BOSOM*.

The RICH man also died and was buried. ²³And finding himself in **torment** in the underworld, he lifted up his eyes and sees ABRAHAM far off and *LAZARUS* (lying) in his *BOSOM*. ²⁴And he called out, "Father ABRAHAM, have compassion on me, and send *LAZARUS* to dip the end of his finger in water and cool my tongue, for I am *suffering pain* in these flames."

²⁵But ABRAHAM said, "My child, remember that in your lifetime you received good things and *LAZARUS* received evil things. But now he is comforted here, and you are *suffering pain*.

²⁶"And besides, a great gulf has been fixed between us and you, so that those who want to pass from here to you cannot, nor can they who would cross from there to us."

²⁷[Secondary interpretation] And he said, "Then I beg you, father, to send him to my father's house ²⁸where I have five brothers, so that he may testify to them, lest they also come to this place of **torment**."

²⁹But ABRAHAM said, "They have ***Moses and the prophets***; let them *heed* them."

³⁰And he said to him, "They won't do that, father ABRAHAM, but if someone came to them *from the dead*, they would repent."

³¹But he said to him, "If they do not *heed* ***Moses and the prophets***, neither will they be convinced if someone should rise *from the dead*."

ARGUMENT AGAINST AUTHENTICITY

The story consists of two parts, verses 19b–25 and verses 27–31.

The first part of the story, which tells of compensation for earthly fortunes in a life to come, has countless parallels in the ancient popular literature and wisdom. The figure of Abraham makes it probable that the story originated in Judaism. Its intent is both to comfort the poor and to warn the rich. Attention to the poor is an especially characteristic emphasis in Luke's Gospel (Luke 1:53; 3:11; 4:18; 6:20; 12:13–21; 14:12–14, 33; 16:1–13, 19–31). The theme of the rejection of the rich is a fingerprint of Luke's editorial activity (Luke 6:24).

The second part of this story concerns the characteristic early Christian theme of the lack of belief in the resurrection of Jesus among Jews. The concluding line (verse 31) refers to Jesus; here in verses 29 and 31 Luke adduces the testimony of Moses and the prophets as he does later in Luke 24:27, 44.

Verse 26 is a Lukan transition to his fabricated second part of the narrative, which in verses 27–31 continues the conversation between the rich man and Abraham begun in verse 24. As the rich man's torment cannot be relieved (for the reason given in verse 26), he asks that Lazarus might at least be sent to warn his five brothers. But Abraham refuses this request, noting that since Moses and the prophets have already made God's will known to the five brothers, the resurrection of a dead man will not be enough to change their ways. Clearly, Luke's formulation alludes to the failure of many Jews to respond to the resurrection of Jesus. And it is equally clear that Luke is intent on identifying that portion of God's will wherein the six wealthy brothers have been remiss. It consists in caring for the poor and giving alms, not being greedy.

As for the historicity of verses 19–25, we are safe in concluding from the many Lukan elements that this passage does not go back to Jesus, and the reference to Jesus' resurrection shows that the same is true for verses 27–31.

Matthew 13:24–30, 37–43

The weeds among the wheat, or an exhortation to be patient

24bThe kingdom of heaven may be likened to someone who sowed good seed in his field. 25But while the people were sleeping, his **enemy** came and sowed WEEDS among the wheat and went away. 26And when the plants began to bear grain, the WEEDS also appeared.

27And the slaves of the householder came and said to him, "Lord, did you not sow good seed in your field? Why then does it now have WEEDS?"

28And he said to them, "An **enemy** has done this."

And the slaves said to him, "Then do you want us to go and gather them?"

29But he said, "No, lest in gathering the WEEDS you also tear up the roots of the wheat. 30Let both grow together until harvest; and at harvest time I will say to the reapers, 'First gather the WEEDS and bind them in bundles to burn them; but gather the wheat into my barn.'"

36[Secondary interpretation] *Then Jesus let the people go and came home. And the disciples came to him and said,* "Interpret to us the parable of the WEEDS in the fields!"

37aHe answered and said:

37bThe one who sows good seed is the SON OF MAN,

38the field is the *world*,

and the good seed are the *sons of the kingdom*.

The WEEDS are the sons of the evil one,

39and the **enemy** who sows them is the *devil*.

The harvest is the end of time,

and the reapers are the *ANGELS*.

40"*Just as the* WEEDS *are collected and burned (up) with fire, so will it be at the end of time.* [41] *The* SON OF MAN *will send his* ANGELS, *and they will pluck from his kingdom all that causes offence and the evildoers.* [42]'They will throw them into the fiery furnace,' [Dan 3:6] where *there will be wailing and grinding of teeth.* [43] *Then the righteous will shine like the sun in the kingdom of their Father.*

"*Whoever has ears ought to hear.*"

ARGUMENT AGAINST AUTHENTICITY

Matt 13:24–30: This parable, a variant of which appears in Thomas 57, stands in place of the parable of the seed growing by itself in Mark 4:26–30, which Matthew has omitted, probably on purpose. The present narrative shares with Mark's parable the warning against intervening in the process of growth between sowing and harvest. It differs in that it recounts not an everyday occurrence but an unusual individual action, the point of which is that despite the "sowing" of the kingdom of God, evil is still present in the world. In this way the parable reflects experiences of the young community with "the evil one" and calls for patience. "The enemy" in verse 28 euphemistically represents the devil (cf. Mark 4:15), and the parable thus features an allegorical element at this decisive point.

Matt 13:37–43: This interpretation of the parable of the weeds (Matt 13:24–30) hardly goes back to its narrator. First, the interpretation nowhere touches on the key point of the parable, the admonition to patience. Second, the interpretation is selective, since no significance is attached to the people sleeping (verse 25) or the servants and their conversation with the master (verses 27–29) or the barns (verse 30). Third, Matt 13:36–43 is particularly illustrative of Matthew's linguistic peculiarities (the most important examples are printed in italics in the translation).

It follows from these observations that the interpretation derives from another narrator than the "Jesus" of the parable of the weeds, and may well come from Matthew himself, who has ascribed to Jesus his own allegorical deciphering in order to impress upon the members of his community that they still face judgment (cf. Matt 25:31–46) and are therefore summoned to righteousness.

Luke 12:42–46

The watchful and negligent slaves, or an exhortation to dutifulness and justice

⁴¹Peter said, "*LORD* are you telling this parable to us or to all?" ⁴²ᵃAnd the *LORD* said, ⁴²ᵇ"Who, then, is the **faithful** and wise *STEWARD* whom the *LORD* will set over his *SERVANTS*, to give them their portion of food at the proper time? ⁴³Blessed is that *SERVANT* whom his *LORD*, when he comes, will find so doing. ⁴⁴Truly, I say to you, he will set him over all that he has.

⁴⁵"But if that *SERVANT* says to himself, 'My *LORD* is delayed in coming,' and begins to beat the male *SERVANTS* and the female *SERVANTS*, and to eat and drink and get drunk, ⁴⁶the *LORD* of that *SERVANT* will come on a day when he does not expect (it) and at an hour he does not know, and will cut him in two and give him his portion among the **unfaithful**."

ARGUMENT AGAINST AUTHENTICITY

The parable of the householder comes from Q (cf. Matt 24:45–51). Luke's inserted dialogue between Peter and Jesus (verses 41–42a) gives it a different context from that in Q; in verse 42b Luke substitutes "steward" for "servant" and thus relates it to the leader of the community.

When leaders of the early Christian movement saw that expectations of Jesus' early return were causing anxiety and even disaffection, they developed stories like this to strengthen the faith and resolve of any whose faith might be wavering. But these narrative exhortations to stand fast, be prepared, and the like bear little resemblance to anything that Jesus would have said.

Matthew 25:1–13
The wise and the foolish virgins, or an admonition to be ready

[1]Then the kingdom of heaven is to be compared to ten virgins who took their lamps and WENT OUT TO MEET the **bridegroom**.

[2]And five of them were foolish, and five were wise. [3]For when the foolish took their lamps, they took no oil with them. [4]But the wise took vessels of oil along with their lamps. [5]Now when the **bridegroom** was delayed, they slumbered and slept.

[6]But at midnight there was a cry, "Look, the **bridegroom** is coming! GO OUT TO MEET him!"

[7]Then all those virgins arose and trimmed their lamps.

[8]But the foolish said to the wise, "Give us some of your oil, for our lamps are going out."

[9]But the wise replied, "No, for there will not be enough for us and you; go rather to the dealers and buy for yourselves."

[10]And while they went to buy, the **bridegroom** came, and those who were ready went in with him to the marriage feast; and the door was shut.

[11]But later the other virgins came and say, "**Lord, Lord**, open (the door) for us!" [12]But he replied and said, "Truly, I say to you, I do not know you.

[13]"Watch out therefore, for you know neither the day nor the hour."

ARGUMENT AGAINST AUTHENTICITY

The narrative of the wise and foolish virgins is a mixture of parable and allegory. A pure parable would have led us to expect a mention of the bride who was being married to the bridegroom. But here the believers—represented by the virgins who are waiting for the Messiah—have taken the place of the bride. To this degree it can be said that the present narrative reflects the theme of the delay of the second coming.

Verse 13 is a secondary conclusion with a general warning to watch out. Note that in the parable watching out (as opposed to falling asleep) is not significant; instead readiness for a longer waiting period is what matters.

The narrative is inauthentic since the semi-allegorical form derives from the needs of the members of the community who are intended to find themselves in the parable, which clearly alludes to the delay of the coming of Christ, who was often seen as the church's "bridegroom."

The parable also fits Matthew's oft-repeated theme of separating the sheep from the goats (Matt 25:31–46), the wheat from the weeds (Matt 13:24–30), and the good from the evil (Matt 13:37–43). Here his trope is distinguishing those worthy of being admitted to the wedding banquet from those who are not prepared (on this point see also Matt 22:2–14).

25

Literal or Contextual Distortions of Authentic Sayings

The examples that follow show how, in order to adjust to new situations, actual sayings of Jesus were changed.

A) SPIRITUALIZING OF THE BLESSING OF THE POOR

Luke 6:20b [authentic]

"Blessed are you poor, for yours is the kingdom of God!"

Matthew 5:3 [inauthentic]

"Blessed are the poor in spirit, for theirs is the kingdom of heaven!"

B) THE ETHICAL INTERPRETATION OF THE BLESSING OF THE POOR

Luke 6:21a [authentic]

"Blessed are you who hunger now, for you shall be satisfied!"

Matthew 5:6 [inauthentic]

"Blessed are they who hunger and thirst for righteousness, for they shall be filled!"

C) SPECIFYING THE PROHIBITION OF DIVORCE

Mark 10:11 [authentic]

"Whoever puts away his wife and marries another commits adultery against her."

Matthew 19:9 [inauthentic]

"Whoever divorces his wife, except for adultery, and marries another, commits fornication."

D) THE INTERPRETATION OF THE PARABLE OF THE SOWER

Mark 4:3–8 [authentic]
The parable of the sower

³Listen! A **sower** went out to **sow**. ⁴And it happened that while he was **sowing**

[1] some seed fell on the pathway, and the birds came and devoured it.

[2] ⁵And some fell on rocky ground, where it did not have much earth, and it immediately sprang up because of the lack of deep earth. ⁶But when the sun rose, it was scorched; and because of the lack of a root, it withered.

[3] ⁷And some fell among thorns, and the thorns grew up and choked it, and it bore no fruit.

[4] ⁸But some fell on good earth and bore fruit, growing and increasing and yielding thirty, sixty, and a hundredfold.

ARGUMENT IN FAVOR OF AUTHENTICITY

This parable no doubt reflects the future expectation of Jesus. I classify it with the parables about the kingdom of God. Though the kingdom is not explicitly mentioned, we see the structural contrast that assigns the beginning of the parable to a different point in time from that described by the end: first the sowing is depicted, and in the final verse it is harvest time. Implicitly compared with this is the breaking in of the kingly rule of God, which is likewise confronted with various forms of failure and resistance in the present. In this way the parable calls for hope. Despite all failure and resistance, God produces a glorious result from chancy beginnings. The parable thus expresses a confidence that must have seemed dubious when the kingdom of God did not immediately appear.

Mark 4:14–20 [inauthentic]
The interpretation of the parable of the sower

¹⁴"The sower sows the *word*.

[1] ¹⁵"And these are the ones on the pathway where the *word* is sown: when they hear, Satan immediately comes and takes away the *word* that has been sown in them.

[2] [16]"And these are those who are sown on the rocks: when they hear the *word*, immediately receive it with joy, [17]but have no roots in themselves, for they are people of the moment. When affliction or persecution for the *word*'s sake arises, they stumble.

[3] [18]"And others are those sown in the thorns. These are those who hear the *word*, [19]but then the cares of this *world*, and the deceit of riches, and the desire for other things enter them and choke the *word*, and it fails to yield.

[4] [20]"And these are the ones sown on good earth: they who hear and receive the *word* and bear fruit, thirty, sixty, and a hundredfold."

ARGUMENT AGAINST AUTHENTICITY

This interpretation of the sower is indelibly stamped with Christian terminology. For example, the term "the word" is a characteristic designation widely used in the primitive church to indicate the gospel message. In keeping with this, the text contains several statements about the word that are alien to Jesus' preaching but common in a later period: the preacher spreads the word; the word is received with joy; persecution arises because of the word; the word becomes offensive; the word grows; the word brings forth fruit.

A second reason why this interpretation of the parable cannot go back to Jesus is that words occurring in this text do not appear elsewhere in the first three gospels, but are common in later New Testament literature: two striking examples are "sow" in the sense of "proclaim" and "root" used to signify inner steadfastness.

In addition to these linguistic points, it is crucial to note that the interpretation of the parable does not match the original story, for the seed that was originally the word sown on different kinds of ground has now become different kinds of people. Furthermore, the parable has been shifted in a psychological direction, for it now bears an admonition to the newly converted to examine their hearts to see whether they have been truly converted.

One is therefore compelled to conclude that Mark 4:14–20, the interpretation of the parable of the sower, comes from the primitive church, which saw this parable as an allegory and expounded it accordingly, feature by feature. The seed is the gospel message preached by the early church, and a somewhat awkwardly expressed metaphor presents four types of soil as four kinds of people. Clearly, two quite different images result: gospel message as God's seed, and human beings as God's field.

E) VARIOUS INTERPRETATIONS OF THE PARABLE
OF THE UNJUST STEWARD

Luke 16:1b–7

The parable of the unjust steward [authentic]

1bThere was a rich person who had a steward, and charges were brought to him that this man was swindling him.

2And he called him and said to him, "What is this that I hear about you? Prepare for an audit of your accounts, for you can no longer be my steward."

3And the steward said to himself, "What shall I do? For my **master** is taking the stewardship away from me. I can no longer dig, and I am ashamed to beg. 4I know what I can do so that when I am removed from the stewardship, people will welcome me into their houses."

5And he called his **master's** debtors one by one, and said to the first, "How much do you owe my **master?**"

6Now he said, "One hundred gallons of olive oil."

Now he said to him, "Take your bill and sit down and quickly write fifty."

7Then he said to another, "Now you, how much do you owe?"

He said, "One hundred bushels of wheat."

He told him, "Take your bill and write eighty."

ARGUMENT IN FAVOR OF AUTHENTICITY

It is very probable that the parable goes back to Jesus. Since it is clearly offensive (as the subsequent interpretations will show) and several attempts have been made to mitigate that quality, the criteria of offensiveness and growth apply to it. Indeed, at least five accretions of tradition have been added to verses 1b–7: verse 8a, verse 8b, verse 9, verses 10–12, and verse 13.

I find doubtful the eschatological interpretation of the parable, which sees it as an exhortation to use one's time wisely in view of an imminent catastrophe. Rather, the point of the parable seems to be the wisdom of preparing oneself to deal with insurmountable crises. The resolute use of the present as a precondition for an enjoyable future together with a clear-eyed assessment of circumstances are the two primary lessons inculcated by the story of the steward. But the right use of riches is certainly not a third. One might even see the story as a survival strategy of a reprobate hero, a category that to a degree included Jesus himself (Luke 7:34) as well as hearers like toll collectors and prostitutes, and that appears in other parables (see, e. g., Thomas 98; Matt 13:44 and Luke 18:2–5).

Luke 16:8–13
Various interpretations of the parable of the dishonest steward [inauthentic]

[1] ⁸ᵃ"And the **master** commended the dishonest steward for acting wisely.

[2] ⁸ᵇ"For the sons of this world are wiser in the world's ways than are the sons of light.

[3] ⁹"And I tell you, use UNRIGHTEOUS *mammon* to make yourself friends, so that when it fails they will offer you a permanent home.

[4] ¹⁰"The person who is **faithful** in a very little is also **faithful** in much; and the person who is UNRIGHTEOUS in a very little is also UNRIGHTEOUS in much. ¹¹If then you are not **faithful** in matters of dishonest *mammon*, who will entrust you with true riches? ¹²And if you are not **faithful** in what is another's, who will give you what is your own?

[5] ¹³ᵃ"No servant can *be a slave* to two masters; for either he will hate the one and love the other, or he will be devoted to the one and despise the other. ¹³ᵇYou cannot *be a slave* to both God and ***mammon***."

ARGUMENT AGAINST AUTHENTICITY

Verse 8a [1]: The post-Easter Christian interpretation of the parable begins with this verse and not with verse 8b. It is unlikely that the master would have commended the unjust steward for cheating on him. From now on, the lord Jesus Christ, called "the master" (in Greek *ho kyrios*), is speaking. Note the parallel situation in Luke 18:6, where Jesus similarly interprets a parable in which the main character is designated "dishonest judge," just as the main character of the parable 16:1–7 is named "the dishonest steward" (verse 8). Probably both parables came down to Luke with an application already appended.

Verse 8b [2]: As a new interpretation, this verse develops verse 8a and depicts the steward as a model of shrewdness for believers who must live in a world that honors and even requires shrewdness.

Verse 9 [3]: This verse, in which "Jesus" gives further advice about being accepted into heaven through money, provides yet another interpretation. Note the way in which "welcome into their houses" (verse 4) and "offer a permanent home" (verse 9) correspond. Any natural dislike for the dishonest steward (verse 8a) is overcome to some degree by the fact that the unrighteous mammon (verse 9) can at least provide for a permanent habitation. The narrative of the rich man and poor Lazarus (Luke 16:19–31) will later continue the theme of mammon (= wealth) and make it clear what a rich man has to expect if he does not use his wealth to earn the approbation of both God and man—as implied in verse 9.

Verses 10–12 [4]: These verses are an appendix made up of various sayings that above all seek to prevent the possible misunderstanding that fraud might somehow be commendable in a steward. Cf. verse 10 with Luke 19:17, which contains an antithetical proverb on faithfulness in the smallest things. The proverb in verses 11–12, applied to mammon and eternal goods, holds up the steward not as a model but a malefactor!

Verse 13 [5]: This is an editorial conclusion from the passage. The warning against serving two masters similarly occurs at Matt 6:24 and Thomas 47:2. By inserting "servant" Luke makes specific what Matthew and Thomas formulate as a general principle.

26

Divine Status of Jesus

Matthew 11:28–30
Wisdom's invitation

²⁸"Come to me all who labor and are heavy laden,
and I will give you rest.
²⁹Take my yoke upon you and learn from me;
for I am gentle and lowly in heart,

    and you will find rest for your souls. [Jer 6:16]

³⁰For my yoke is easy and my burden is light."

ARGUMENT AGAINST AUTHENTICITY

These verses are known as the Comfortable Words. Numerous parallels to them appear in the wisdom books: Prov 8:1–21; Sirach 51:23–29 LXX, etc. The words "gentle" and "lowly in heart" carry an ethical significance in the First Gospel, cf. Matt 5:5, 7; 21:5.

The passage presupposes the identification of Jesus with "wisdom" and thus a post-Easter situation, when Christians transferred to their Lord what in pre-Christian times Jews said about Wisdom. The capital letter operates similarly in the two cases. In essence, this equation corresponds to that of Jesus with the Word (in Greek, *logos*) in John 1:1: "In the beginning was the Word, and the Word was with God, and the Word was God." These later formulations are similar to those in Matt 11:28–30.

Matthew 11:25–27
The unanimity of Father and Son

²⁵"I praise you, *Father*, Lord of heaven and earth, because you have hidden all this from the wise and intelligent and REVEALED it to babes. ²⁶Yes, *Father*, for this was your gracious will.

²⁷All things have been given to me by my *Father*,
and no one knows the Sᴏɴ except the *Father*,
and no one knows the *Father* except the Sᴏɴ,
and the one to whom the Sᴏɴ chooses to ʀᴇᴠᴇᴀʟ him."

ARGUMENT AGAINST AUTHENTICITY

Verses 25–27: This section comes from Q (it corresponds to Luke 10:21–22). Since verses 25–26 include a paraphrase of Ps 8:2, they were not likely coined by Jesus; besides, Paul elaborates a similar theme in 1 Cor 1:18–31. In verse 27 Jesus' activity is expressed in the customary style of the revelation-discourse. The words are not authentic because they presuppose the post-Easter situation: compare the words of the "risen" Jesus in Matt 28:18 ("All authority . . . has been given to me") with verse 27 ("All things have been given to me").

John 5:19b–24

*Jesus' authority comes from
his unity with God*

¹⁹ᵇ"Tʀᴜʟʏ, ᴛʀᴜʟʏ, I sᴀʏ ᴛᴏ ʏᴏᴜ,
the Sᴏɴ can do nothing of his own accord,
but only what he sees the *Father* doing.
For whatever he does,
the Sᴏɴ also does likewise.
²⁰ᵃFor the *Father* loves the Sᴏɴ
and shows him all that he himself is doing.
²⁰ᵇAnd greater works than these will he show him, so that you may marvel.
²¹For as the *Father* raises the dead and makes (them) alive,
so also the Sᴏɴ makes alive whom he will.
²²Nor does the *Father judge* anyone,
but he has given all *judgment* to the Sᴏɴ,
²³ᵃthat all may *ʜᴏɴᴏʀ* the Sᴏɴ
as they *ʜᴏɴᴏʀ* the *Father*.

23b Whoever does not HONOR the SON does not HONOR the *Father*
WHO HAS SENT HIM.

24 "TRULY, TRULY, I SAY TO YOU that whoever hears my words
and believes him WHO HAS SENT ME has eternal life and does not
come into *judgment*, but has passed from death to life."

ARGUMENT AGAINST AUTHENTICITY

The elevated style and the change from third to first person
in verse 24 suggest that verses 19b–23 are based on a tradition. It forms a hymn of praise in two strophes, which in
the descriptive present announce the dignity of the exalted
Son in unity with the Father. Here it should be noted that
the hymn expresses a view that has developed far beyond
primitive Christian apocalyptic, for no longer do we read of a
judgment at the last day, nor of a general resurrection of the
dead. Rather, the judgment is given in the present, and not
all are saved, but only those to whom the Son grants eternal
life (cf. verse 21).

Because the tradition contained in verses 19–23a is a
product of theological reflection after Easter, it does not go
back to Jesus.

Verses 20b and 23b can be identified as additions. Verse
20b is formulated in prose and harks back to the miracle
in John 5:2–9 ("greater works than these," cf. John 1:50;
14:12); with the address to the hearers ("that you may marvel") it presupposes an actual or ritualized conversation.
Verse 23b (cf. Luke 10:16b) stands out from what goes before by the change of subject and the sending formula typical
of the Fourth Evangelist.

Verse 24 is a key formulation by the Fourth Evangelist.
Here, as in John 6:47 and 11:25–26, he sums up his new
eschatology: salvation and doom are decided not at the end
of days, but in the present.

John 10:27–30
Warrant of eternal life

[27]"My sheep hear my voice, and I know them, and they follow me, [28]and I give them eternal life, and they shall never perish, and no one will *snatch them* OUT OF MY HAND.

[29]"My Father, who has given (them) to me, is greater than all, and no one can *snatch them* OUT OF THE FATHER'S HAND.

[30]"I and the Father are one."

ARGUMENT AGAINST AUTHENTICITY

The sayings in verses 27–29 are part of Jesus' so-called "shepherd discourse" (John 10:1–18). They are based on the view that Jesus' charge is to assemble around himself a group of believers (the sheep given to him by God) and to lead them to eternal life. However typical and comforting such a thought may have been for those of the Fourth Gospel's intended audience, it was entirely alien to the historical Jesus.

The same conclusion is true for the next saying, verse 30, in which, as in the prologue (John 1:18) and the confession of Thomas in John 20:28 ("My Lord and my God"), Jesus emphasizes his equivalence with God.

John 12:44–50
In Jesus God is present

[44]"Whoever **believes** in me, **believes** not in me but in him WHO HAS SENT ME. [45]And he who sees me sees him WHO HAS SENT ME. [46]I have come as light into the world, in order that whoever **believes** in me may not abide in darkness.

[47]"And if anyone hears *my sayings* and does not observe them, I do not JUDGE him, for I did not come to JUDGE the world, but to save the world.

[48a]"Whoever rejects me and does not receive *my sayings* has a JUDGE; [48b]on the last day the word that I have spoken will JUDGE him.

⁴⁹"For I have not spoken on my own accord; but **the Father WHO HAS SENT ME** has himself commanded me what to say and what to speak. ⁵⁰And I know that his commandment is eternal life. What I now say, then, is what **the Father** has directed me to say."

ARGUMENT AGAINST AUTHENTICITY

There is no connection between this passage and the summary of Jesus' public activity that precedes it (John 12:37–43). Besides, nothing in the present section indicates where, when, or to whom he is speaking. Either he is addressing the readers of the Fourth Gospel or he is talking into thin air. This passage apparently seeks to give a brief summary of the public teaching of Jesus by a selective adoption of individual notions from John 1–12.

Verses 44–46: The first two verses are parallel formulations. Verse 44b has a negative equivalent in John 5:23; verse 45 has considerable similarity with John 14:9. Verse 46 recalls above all John 3:19–21, but also John 1:4–10; 9:5; 12:35–36.

Verse 47: The expression "observe [my sayings]" in verse 47a does not occur elsewhere in the Gospel of John (instead it is always "keep"); verse 47b echoes John 3:16.

Verse 48a: The word "reject" is unique in the Gospel of John (but cf. Luke 10:16); "has a judge" (literally, "has one [who] judges him") recalls John 8:50 ("there is [one] who . . . judges") and first suggests God as judge.

Verse 48b: But the verse continues with two surprising statements: first, that the *word* spoken by Jesus has the function of judging, and second, that it will exercise this function on the *last day*. The first notion looks like an attempt to draw a balance between sayings in which Jesus speaks of himself as a judge (John 5:22, 27, 30; 8:16) and those according to which Jesus has not come to judge but to save the world (especially the above-noted repetition of 3:16 in verse 47b).

With "on the last day" the second notion recalls the same phrase in John 6:39, 40c, 44c, 54—verses that a scholarly consensus understands to have been added later. Just as their notion of the resurrection "on the last day" clashes with the notion that the believer is already in possession of eternal life, so here the assertion of judgment "on the last day" is in conflict with the view put forward in John 3:18 that the one who does not believe has already been judged.

Verses 49–50: These verses are similar to John 3:1; 5:19; 8:26, 28, 38, 40.

This section is a secondary literary product and does not contain authentic sayings of Jesus.

27

"I am" Sayings

John 6:35b, 48–51
Bread of Life

35b"*I am the* BREAD *of life;*
whoever comes to me shall not hunger,
and whoever believes in me shall never thirst. . . .

48I am the BREAD of life. 49Our ancestors ate the manna in the wilderness, and they died.

50This is the BREAD *that comes down from heaven,*
that one may eat of it and not die.

51aI am the living BREAD *that came down from heaven.*
Whoever eats of this BREAD will live forever,
51band the BREAD that I will give is my flesh for the life of the world."

ARGUMENT AGAINST AUTHENTICITY

The "I am" saying in verses 35 and 48 bears formal resemblance to those in John 8:12 and 14:6—all three are sayings from the tradition—and substantive similarity to John 7:37b–38a. It promises that believers will overcome earthly mortality, and does so using terminology that especially recalls Jewish wisdom literature and apocalyptic texts. See, for example, Sir 24:21—"Whoever eats of me [= wisdom], always hungers for me; and whoever drinks of me, always thirsts for me"—and Isa 49:10—"They will neither hunger nor thirst" (cf. also Matt 5:6; Rev 7:16).

Note that the motif of thirst plays no role in the context. To derive this probably traditional saying from the historical Jesus, one must presuppose that Jesus thought the fullness of salvation to be preeminently present in his person. This presupposition is in direct conflict with Gospel passages in which Jesus subordinates himself to God (cf. Mark 10:18) and characterizes himself as one still waiting for the full advent of salvation (cf. Matt 6:10). The reverse assumption—that these passages from Mark and Matthew are secondary and the attributions stamped by John's high Christology are primary—must surely be rejected, for it is clear that the trend of early Christian theology was not to reduce the importance of Jesus. Quite the contrary, his person was increasingly made divine. Therefore, John 6:35b and the other "I am" sayings in the Fourth Gospel stem from people who after Easter came to believe in the divinity of Jesus.

The words that follow John 6:35b are intended to make Jesus' claim to be the bread of life more explicit. Verses 48–51b round off the section. Here the truth expressed without an image in verse 47—"whoever believes has eternal life"—is given dramatic emphasis by repeating the bread metaphor from verses 31–35.

Verse 51b introduces a jarring note with its assertion of the necessity of the Eucharist for salvation. This is especially puzzling since, as was noted earlier, the Fourth Gospel elsewhere displays an indifferent if not a critical attitude toward cultic sacramental piety, and the Johannine account of the Last Supper (chapter 13) omits the Pauline and synoptic report of the institution of the Eucharist. In addition, verses 51b–58 represent an alien element in the context of chapter 6 (see further above, pp. 50–52).

John 8:12b

Light of the World

"I am the light of the world.
Whoever follows me
will not walk in darkness,
but will have the light of life."

ARGUMENT AGAINST AUTHENTICITY

Against the authenticity of this saying the same objections apply as were raised against the authenticity of the saying in John 6:35b. An additional problem is that the opposition between light and darkness was not a theme employed in the preaching of the historical Jesus, but is rather a concept typical of the Fourth Gospel (see John 1:5; 3:19; 12:35–36).

John 10:7b–10

Sheep and Door

7b"Truly, truly, I say to you,
    I am the **door** of the sheepfold.
8All who preceded me are thieves and robbers, but the sheep did not listen to them.
    9I am the **door**;
    if anyone enters by me
    he will be saved,
    and will go in and go out
    and find pasture.
10The thief does not come
    except to steal and kill and destroy;
I have come
    in order that they may have life, and have it abundantly."

ARGUMENT AGAINST AUTHENTICITY

This passage exhibits badly mixed metaphors. While in verses 7b and 9 Jesus compares himself with the "door", verses 8 and 10 reflect his identification as the "good shepherd," a designation that becomes explicit only in verse 11. Not only do the images not match, but if Jesus is the "door" then the notion that others (prophets? Pharisees?) have preceded him (verse 8) is clumsy. Hence, one must assume that the idea of Jesus as the door was added at a later stage of composition and that therefore the passage is inauthentic.

The theologian responsible for these additions has taken a minor aspect of the preceding allegory (10:1–5)—the door—and used it to paint Jesus as the sole way to salvation (cf. John 14:6). The following sayings about Jesus the good shepherd are therefore older, but they are equally inauthentic.

John 10:11–16
Good Shepherd

¹¹"I AM THE GOOD **SHEPHERD**.

The good shepherd LAYS DOWN HIS LIFE FOR THE SHEEP.

¹²The hired servant, who is not a **SHEPHERD**, to whom the sheep do not belong, sees the wolf coming and leaves the sheep and flees—and the wolf snatches them and scatters them—¹³for he is a hired servant and does not care for the sheep.

¹⁴I AM THE GOOD **SHEPHERD**,

and I *know* my own

and my own *know* me,

¹⁵as the FATHER *knows* me

and I *know* the FATHER;

and I LAY DOWN MY LIFE FOR THE SHEEP.

¹⁶And I have other sheep that are not of this fold; them also I must lead, and they will listen to my voice, and there will be one flock, one **SHEPHERD**."

ARGUMENT AGAINST AUTHENTICITY

Verse 11: This verse for the first time explicitly makes the identification of Jesus with the shepherd—an identification that is doubtless intended in verses 1b–5 and already envisioned in verses 8 and 10. However, a good shepherd has not been mentioned in verses 1b–5, for there the contrast was not between good and a bad shepherd but between the shepherd and the thieves.

Verse 11b: The announcement that the good shepherd gives his life for the sheep (= Jesus for his own) goes beyond verses 1b–5. In this imagery the shepherd's readiness for death is an extreme exaggeration that is clearly a retrospective allusion to the death of Jesus.

Verses 12–13: These verses draw a contrast with the shepherd's readiness for sacrifice, and have no more a basis in verses 1b–5 than does verse 11b. For neither the hired servant nor the wolf plays a role there. So it is no wonder that the overall picture becomes increasingly blurred. Whereas in verse 10 the thief threatens the sheep, according to verse 12 the danger comes from the wolf. And whereas in verse 5 the sheep flee from a stranger, now it is the hired servant who takes flight before the wolf.

Verses 14–15: Verse 14a corresponds to verse 11a. Verses 14b–15a echo the remarks in verse 3 about knowing the voice of the shepherd and calling the sheep by name. The view that the relationship between Father and Son corresponds to the relationship between Jesus and the community is typical of the revisers of this Gospel (cf. John 6:56–57 and 17:20–21).

Verse 16: This verse interrupts the connection between verses 15 and 17, and together with the abrupt mention of the other sheep, whose existence has not previously been indicated, completely destroys the cohesion of the image. The real purpose of this verse is to introduce the new notion that the church is composed not only of Jewish Christians but also of Gentile Christians. However, such a distinction is alien to the context, since in it the shepherd's "own sheep" represent the totality of all Christians. As this differentiation is also expressed in the additions John 11:51–52 and 17:20–21, we may reasonably conjecture that all three additions derive from one and the same individual or group.

The announcement that the good shepherd gives his life for the sheep—signifying Jesus' readiness to die for the sake of his followers—is post-Easter hyperbole. Further, since verse 16 indicates a church that is composed not only of

Jewish Christians but also of Gentile Christians, the passage clearly dates to a time after Jesus' death.

John 11:25b–26
Resurrection and Life

25b"I am the resurrection and the life;
whoever *believes* in me, even if he dies, shall live,
26and whoever lives and *believes* in me shall never die."

ARGUMENT AGAINST AUTHENTICITY

This "I am" saying underscores the cherished thought of the Fourth Gospel that the believer already possesses eternal life. In addition, it shows that the certainty of the life thus received includes a salvation that extends beyond the death of the individual: Jesus saves the believer's life from any and all threats of death (cf. John 12:32).

Among the serious difficulties of this passage is that it renders the preceding account of the raising of Lazarus superfluous, and indeed robs of all significance an episode for which it ostensibly forms the conclusion. For that miracle story deals not with eternal life but with the resuscitation of a corpse; further, it does not indicate that Lazarus believed in Jesus. In short, it seems that the author must have created this brief passage and inserted it without recognizing its inconsistency with the preceding narrative. At any rate, the statement that Jesus is the resurrection and the life presupposes the conviction that Jesus himself has risen. Since that belief cannot be assigned to his lifetime, the saying cannot be authentic.

John 14:4–7
Way, Truth, Life

4"And where I am going, you are acquainted with the WAY."

5Thomas says to him, "Master, we are not acquainted with where you are going; how can we be acquainted with the WAY?"

6Jesus says to him,

"I am the WAY and the truth and the life;

no one comes to the *Father*, but by ME.

[7]And if you have *known* ME, then you will *know* my *Father* also. And even now you *know* him and see him."

ARGUMENT AGAINST AUTHENTICITY

Verse 4: This verse is a rather contrived lead-in to the theme of the "way", which hitherto has played no role.

Verse 5: The disciples, who here are represented by Thomas (cf. John 11:16; 20:24–29), do not understand Jesus' remarks and this offers Jesus an occasion to explain the mystery of the "way" (for the motif of the disciples' incomprehension, cf. 2:20).

Verse 6: This "I am Saying" most probably derives from tradition (cf. John 6:35; concerning the claim to exclusiveness cf. Exod 20:2–3; Acts 4:12); note that in the present context only the term "way" is significant, since Jesus' identification of himself with the "truth" and the "life" is left unnoticed. And since verse 6 discloses the meaning of verse 4, it is clear that Jesus has not been speaking about his own way into the house of the Father, but about the way of the disciples. For them, Jesus himself is the exclusive way to God.

This passage makes two important claims: that Jesus is the sole source of salvation (cf. verse 6; see Acts 4:12), and that God is present in Jesus (verse 7). Both statements are basic for the theology of the Fourth Gospel, yet both derive from and are dependent upon the resurrection of Jesus. The historical Jesus cannot have spoken these words.

John 15:1–8
the Vine

[1]"I am the true **vine**,

and *my Father* is the vine-dresser.

²Every branch in me that does not BEAR FRUIT he removes,
  and every (branch) that bears fruit he prunes that it may BEAR
  more FRUIT.
    ³You have already been made clean by the word that I have
    spoken to you.
⁴ABIDE in me
  and I (abide) in you.
As the branch cannot BEAR FRUIT by itself
  unless it ABIDES in the vine,
neither can you
  unless you ABIDE in me.
⁵I am the vine,
  you (are) the branches.
Whoever ABIDES in me and I in him
  BEARS much FRUIT, because without me you can do nothing.
⁶Whoever does not ABIDE in me
  is cast out like prunings and withers; and they gather them
  and cast them into the fire, and they burn.
    ⁷"If you ABIDE in me and my words ABIDE in you, (then) ask
whatever you will, and it will be done for you. ⁸In this *my Father* is
glorified, that you BEAR much FRUIT, and prove to be my disciples."

ARGUMENT AGAINST AUTHENTICITY

The discourse about the true vine springs directly from
Hebrew Bible motifs (cf. e.g. Isa 5:1–7; Jer 2:21; 6:9; Ezek
15:1–8; 17:1–10; 19:10–14; Hos 10:1; Sir 24:17–18; see
also Matt 15:13). Its admonition to abide in Christ and
thereby to live a fruitful life includes the promise that those
who do so will be rewarded (verse 7) and the threat of judgment upon those who do not (verses 2a, 6). Several incon-
sistencies indicate that the author based this sub-section on
an earlier simile:

(a) The statement about the "cleanness" of the disciples
in verse 3, which recalls John 13:10b, renders superfluous
the pruning activity of the vine-dresser (= God) spoken of in
verse 2b.

(b) Verse 4 contains the only imperative within the subsection and anticipates the identification of the branches with the community of disciples, a trope that is made explicit only in verse 5. Moreover, the frequent occurrence of the verb "abide" is suspicious, as the author also uses this term several times in verses 9–11, which certainly came from him.

(c) The broad depiction of the judgment in verse 6 gives the impression that the "remove" of verse 2a was not drastic enough for the author. Furthermore, verse 6b introduces an undefined group of people, and thus conflicts with the first part of the image, which is focused on vine, vinedresser and branches.

(d) Verse 7 similarly confuses the picture; evidently John 14:13 prompted the promise of response to prayer and the following statement about the glorification of the Father.

Yet neither can that older simile be ascribed to the historical Jesus. Rather, it must be seen as the word of a prophet who was so concerned about retaining the loyalty of his community that he claimed to speak in the name of the exalted Christ. The verb "to abide" (for present contextual examples see John 15:4, 5, 6, 7) in the sense of "to abide in Christ (or in God)" makes numerous appearances in 1 John (2:6, 24, 27–28; 3:6, 24, etc.). No doubt this is because the author had to deal with divisions within the Johannine community (see 1 John 2:18–19; 4:1–3).

28

Prayers

Mark 14:32–42
Prayer at Gethsemane

³²And they *COME* to a garden the name of which (is) Gethsemane.

And he says to his disciples, "Sit here until I have PRAYED." ³³And he takes Peter, James, and John with him and began to tremble in distress ³⁴and says to them, "My soul is troubled to death; remain here and ***watch***."

³⁵And he went a little further, threw himself on the ground and PRAYED that if it was possible, the HOUR might pass by him; ³⁶and he said, "Abba, Father, all is possible for you, take this cup from me; yet not what I will but what you (will)."

³⁷And he *COMES* and finds them **sleeping** and says to Peter, "Simon, are you **asleep**? Could you not keep ***watch*** one HOUR? ³⁸***Watch*** and PRAY, that you do not fall into temptation. The spirit is willing but the flesh is weak."

³⁹And he went away again and PRAYED, saying the same words. ⁴⁰And again he came and found them **sleeping**; for their eyes were very heavy, and they did not know what to answer him.

⁴¹And he *COMES* a third time and says to them, "**Sleep** on and rest! It's all over; the HOUR has come. See, the Son of man is delivered up into the hands of sinners. ⁴²Arise, let us go. Look, the one who is delivering me up is here."

ARGUMENT AGAINST AUTHENTICITY

In order to understand the text rightly we must cancel the presumption that the narrator is a conscientious historian. Such a notion overlooks the stated fact that no one else was present during Jesus' prayerful struggle in Gethsemane. Rather, we must seek to understand the edifying purpose behind Mark's fiction. The story emphasizes the obedience of the Son of God as opposed to the dullness of the disciples.

Its climax comes in the contrast between Jesus' agonized surrender to God's will (verse 36) and the uncomprehending dereliction of the disciples.

Yet it is noteworthy that a parallel tradition to the Gethsemane scene shows the broader horizon of the thought that underlies it. The writer of Heb 5:7 reports that "In the day of his earthly life [Jesus] offered prayers and weeping with loud cries and tears to the one who could save him from death; and he was heard for his godly fear." This dialectic statement derives from Hebrew Bible psalms that were an important source for the Gethsemane scene in particular, and the passion story in general. In the present instance three passages are worthy of note. Psalm 22:24: God "has not despised nor scorned the misery of the poor and has not hidden his face from him; and when he cried to him, he heard it." Psalm 31:22: "I said in my alarm: I am driven from your sight. But you heard the voice of my weeping when I cried to you." Psalm 69:3: "I have cried myself weary, my throat is parched. My eyes have become dim because I have to wait so long for my God."

The scene in Gethsemane is not intended to disillusion but to aid the auditor or reader in understanding revelation; like the whole of the Mark's passion story its focus is not psychology, but salvation history. Thus the material appropriated from the Hebrew Bible to portray the obedient Son of God was primarily intended to create a contrast to the Markan motif of the cowardly and dull disciples.

The historical value of the Gethsemane account is nil. The one argument occasionally advanced in favor of its historicity, that the section is too offensive christologically to have been invented, quickly comes to grief on the clearly edifying purpose of the passage that was noted at the outset.

The historicity of Jesus' words to the "inner circle" of his disciples is made dubious by the lack of other witnesses and the unlikelihood that they would report their shameful behavior; when he prayed (verse 36) no one else was present. Accordingly, all his speeches in this passage are extremely doubtful or totally fictitious. Since the words addressed to the disciples are part of the story, their value as possible aphorisms or pronouncements is extremely unlikely. One possible exception to this general assessment is "The spirit is willing, but the flesh is weak"—a proverbial saying that might be assigned to almost anyone. The prayer is probably a Markan composition, since verse 35 uses indirect discourse to anticipate it and verse 39 curtly reports its reiteration. Mark or an unknown source called on imagination to create the text.

John 17:1–26
Jesus' farewell prayer

¹. . . Jesus . . . lifted up his eyes to heaven and said,

"Father, the hour has come; glorify your Son so that the Son may glorify you, ²just as you have *given* him authority over all flesh so that he may *give* eternal life to all those whom you have *given* to him. ³And this is eternal life that they **know** you, the only true GOD, and Jesus Christ, whom you SENT.

⁴"I have **glorified** you on earth, having accomplished the work that you have *given* me to do.

⁵"And now, FATHER, **glorify** me with your **glory** that I had with you before the *WORLD* was.

⁶"I have revealed your name to those of the WORLD whom you *gave* me. They were yours, and you have *given* them to me, and they have kept your word. ⁷Now they **know** that everything that you have *given* me is from you. ⁸For I have *given* them the words that you have *given* to me, and they have received them and have come to **know** in truth that I have come forth from you, and have believed that you SENT ME.

⁹"I am praying for them; I am not praying for the *WORLD*, but for those whom you have given me, for they are yours; ¹⁰and all that is mine is yours, and what is yours is mine, and I am **glori-**

fied in them. [11a]And now I am no longer in the WORLD, but they are in the WORLD, and I am coming to you.

[11b]"Holy FATHER, *keep them in your name that you have given me*, that they may be one just as we are one.

[12]"While I was with them *I kept them in your name that you have given me*, and I guarded (them), and none of them perished but the son of perdition, and that was so that the scripture might be fulfilled. [13]But now I am coming to you, and these things I (still) speak in the WORLD that they may have my joy fulfilled in themselves.

[14]"I have *given* them your word, and the WORLD hated them because they do not belong to the WORLD, just as I do not belong to the WORLD. [15]I do not ask you to take them out of the WORLD, but to keep them from evil. [16]They are not of the WORLD, as I am not of the WORLD.

[17]"Sanctify them in the truth. Your word is truth.

[18]"As you SENT ME into the WORLD, so too I SENT THEM into the WORLD. [19]And I sanctify myself for them, so that they too may be sanctified in truth. [20]And not only for these do I pray, but also for those who through their word believe in me, [21]that they may all be one, as you, FATHER, are in me and I in you, so that they also may be in us, so that the WORLD believes that you have SENT ME.

[22]"And I have *given* them the **glory** that you have *given* me, that they may be one, even as we are one, [23]I in them and you in me, so that they may attain perfect unity, so that the WORLD may know that you have sent me, and that you have loved them even as you have loved me.

[24]"Father, I also desire that those you have given me may be where I am so that they see my **glory** which you have *given* me, because you loved me (even) before the foundation of the WORLD.

[25]"Righteous Father, the WORLD has not **known** you, but I have **known** you, and these have come to **know** that you SENT ME. [26]And I have made your name **known** to them, and I will continue to make it **known,** so that the love with which you loved me may be in them, and so I in them."

ARGUMENT AGAINST AUTHENTICITY

This section represents the fourth and last of the additions inserted between John 14:31 and 18:1 (see the introduction to chapters 15–17 above, pp. 69–70). Like all the previous farewell discourses added at a later stage, chapter 17 too has probably been composed specifically for its present context. First, the isolated context of such a prayer would in any case be hard to imagine; and second, it contains a number of references not only to the preceding farewell discourses but also to other parts of the Gospel of John.

Verse 1a: The phrase "Jesus said this" (cf. John 12:36b) clearly marks off the prayer from the preceding discourses.

Verses 1b–2: The motif of the arrival of the hour (of the passion) recalls John 12:23 and 13:1. With the following petition concerning the reciprocal glorification of God and Jesus, the author wants to build a bridge back to 13:31–32, the beginning of the farewell discourses (cf. moreover John 14:13: "that the Father may be glorified in the Son"). This is also suggested by the fact that here, as in John 13:31–32, Jesus speaks of himself in the third person, whereas from verse 4 onward he will use the first person. Verse 2 makes a vital distinction: certainly Jesus has been given authority (cf. John 5:27) over "all flesh"—a Jewish term for "all human beings"—but he bestows eternal life only on a group chosen by the Father. This group of those entrusted to Jesus is summed up in the formula "those whom you have given to him" (cf. verses 6, 9, 24), which is characteristic of chapter 17.

Verse 3: The content of this verse—which is a later addition—falls outside the substance of the prayer.

Verse 4: Jesus' first report about what he has done was evidently influenced by John 4:34 and 5:36.

Verse 5: The first individual petition concerns Jesus himself, whereas the three following ones (verses 11b, 17, 24) represent intercessions for his own. It corresponds to the basic petition verse 1b (including the address "Father"), but expands this with the notion that the glory of Jesus is to be the same as that which he had in his pre-existence (see John 1:1–3).

Verses 6–8: The second report introduces the notion of the "name" of God (verse 6; cf. John 12:28), a motif that is taken up again both in the petition (verse 11b) and in the concluding reason for it (verse 12a; cf. moreover verse 26a). Again it is emphasized that salvation is limited to those for whom it is predestined by God (cf. on verses 1b–2). For the keeping of the word of God by the disciples (verse 6b) cf. John 8:51, 52, and above all John 14:23–24; cf. 15:20c. The knowledge of the disciples (verse 7) is once again emphasized in verses 8 and 25 (here, in contrast to the lack of knowledge of the world). In literary terms John 16:27 and 11:42 have influenced verse 8.

Verses 9–11a: The introduction to the second petition once again draws a clear line between the world and those entrusted to Jesus: the world is explicitly excluded from Jesus' intercession (verses 9–10). Verse 11 recalls the farewell situation and refers back to John 13:1, 33, 36; 14:2–4, 12, 28; 16:5, 7, 28.

Verse 11b: With the formulation "keep in your name," the petition harks back to the report in verses 6–8. The concluding notion of unity, which is repeated in verse 22b, has a basis in John 10:30, 10:38, and 14:20. The petition that God keep the disciples in his name presupposes the statement of verse 6a that Jesus has revealed his Father's name to those whom the Father has given him. In other words, the disciples should be kept in God's being.

Verses 12a, 13: These verses give the reason for the petition: during his presence on earth Jesus was responsible for keeping the disciples in the name of God. Now that he is leaving the disciples, he must return to God the task of keeping the disciples in his word. The concluding statement about perfect joy recalls John 15:11 (cf. also John 16:20–22, 24).

Verse 14: This report echoes word for word the remarks in the second addition (15:18–16:15) about the hatred of the world (cf. above John 15:19). "I am not of the world" has a parallel in John 8:23.

Verse 15: In its first part, formulated in the negative, the introduction to the third petition picks up verse 14b: despite the world's hatred the disciples are not to be taken out of the world. The positive part bears a similarity to a petition of the Lord's Prayer (cf. Matt 6:13b: "Deliver us from evil!").

Verse 17: The connection between this petition and the 'word' mentioned in the report becomes clearer when one introduces into verse 17a the identification made in verse 17b: the result is "Sanctify them in your word!"

Verses 18–19: These verses form the reason for the petition. Verse 18 bears a great similarity to John 20:21 and is probably dependent on this verse (for the form of the statement cf. also John 15:9). Verse 19 refers back to "sanctify" in verse 17.

Verses 22–23: With the keyword "glory" (verse 22a), the last report and the following petition (verse 24) take up the central term of the basic petition and its first development (verses 1–2a, 4–5: 1x "glory"; 4x "glorify"). This gives the prayer a kind of framework.

Verse 24: In contrast to verses 5, 11b and 17, the petition is formulated not as an imperative but with "I desire." For its content cf. the addition John 12:26; 14:3 (this passage has been used here); 1:14 and 15:9. In connection with the motif of the glory of Jesus, God's love for Jesus before the beginning of time points back to verse 5.

Verses 25–26: These verses form the reason for the last petition. At the same time, by taking up individual motifs from the other developments of the basic petition, they sum up the whole prayer and thus give it a solemn conclusion. For the world's alienation from God noted in verse 25a, cf. John 8:55 (Jesus says to the Jews, "You have not known him, but I know him") and the numerous parallels in the previous farewell discourses (John 14:17, 22; 15:18–25; 16:2–4a, 8–9, 20, 33). Verse 25b corresponds to the end of verse 8b. Verse 26a takes up verse 6 and adds a corresponding future statement (cf. similarly the voice of God in John 12:28). The motif of the love of God for Jesus, coupled with the notion of unity, picks up the end of verse 23.

According to Matt. 6:7 Jesus says, "When you pray, you are not to babble like the Gentiles, for they think that they will be heard for their many words." And while that saying can hardly be deemed authentic, it is still far closer to being a believable saying of the historical Jesus than the numbing spate of words found in John 17. Jesus' farewell prayer is a literary product derived from other elements of the Gospel of John, especially those found in chapters 13–16. It is of no value for those who seek to solve the several enigmas of the historical Jesus.

Conclusion

Fictional Jesus-Sayings and the Quest for Truth

We cannot do anything against the truth,
but only for the truth.

Paul, Ephesians 4:25

Any contemporary person who turns to the New Testament for objective information about Jesus is bound to come away feeling queasy. Although early Christians acclaimed truth as a component of holiness and condemned lying as one of the sins they had supposedly overcome, the utterances attributed to Jesus in the New Testament Gospels are for the most part heavily redacted or wholly invented sayings intended to edify the earliest Christians, many of whom were waiting for Jesus to return from Heaven. Unfortunately, the Church today often proclaims these texts to be the Word of God, even though scholars—many of them committed Christians—long ago discredited them as inauthentic.

It must be remembered, however, that the revisers and inventors were persuaded of the authentic nature of these sayings. Thus they were not acting deceptively, but rather believed that by their actions they were responding to a higher truth. Still, it is beyond question that by today's standards these Christians propagated lies and that, since the lies remain part and parcel of Christianity's received Scriptures, the Church's transmission of falsehood continues unabated.

Clearly, this preponderance of spurious Jesus-sayings gravely undermines any assertions of their religious valid-

119

ity, and obliges the serious reader both to reassess the New Testament Gospels, and to recognize that apart from a relatively small number of authentic reports they are to be valued primarily as museum pieces. Finally, it would seem axiomatic that the search for ultimate truths cannot afford to have its foundations riddled with untruths. Therefore, since these many falsely ascribed sayings remain fundamental elements of the Christian tradition taught in both church and seminary, it seems evident that only a radical and sweeping exegetical reform can save that tradition from increasing irrelevance and eventual self-destruction.

Appendix

Sayings of Jesus in the Letters to the Seven Churches in *Revelation*

As the following letters show, early Christians believed that Jesus' voice remained alive even after his death. The prophetic disciple John (for the name see Rev 1:1, 4, 9; 22) claimed access to the risen Jesus inasmuch as the heavenly Lord had appeared to him during a visionary experience (Rev 1:10; 4:1–2) and charged him to write down seven dictated letters (Rev 1:12–20). The details of these letters include many parallels to passages in the New Testament Gospels, of which the following list is but a brief sampling:

- **Rev 2:4:** "But I have this against you: that you have abandoned your first love."
  Matt 24:12: "Because lawlessness gains the upper hand, the love of many will grow cold."

- **Rev 2:7:** "Whoever has an ear ought to hear".
  Matt 11:15 (parr.): "Whoever has ears to hear ought to hear."

- **Rev 2:10:** "Do not fear what you will suffer. Look, the devil will throw some of you into prison, that you may be tested, and for ten days you will have tribulation. Be faithful unto death, and I will give you the crown of life."
  Matt 10:28 (parr.): "Do not fear those who kill the body but cannot kill the soul. Fear rather the one who can destroy both soul and body in hell."

- **Rev 3:2:** "Watch out!"
  Mark 13:35, 37: "Watch out!"

- **Rev: 3:3b:** "If you do not watch out, I will come like a thief, and you will never know at what hour I will come upon you."
  Matt 24:43 / Luke 12:39: "Know this, that if the householder had known in what watch of the night (in Luke, "hour") the thief was coming…" (Cf. also 1 Thess 5:2; Thomas 21:5; 2 Pet 3:10a).

- **Rev 3:5:** "The victor shall thus be clothed in white garments, I will not blot his name out of the book of life; I will confess his name before my Father and before his angels."
  Luke 10:20a: "Rejoice that your names are written in heaven."
  Luke 12:8 (parr): "Everyone who confesses me before people, the Son of man also will confess before the angels of God."

- **Rev 3:8b:** "You have little strength, and yet you have kept my word and have not denied my name."
  John 8:51: "Truly, truly, I say to you, if anyone keeps my word, he will never see death."

- **Rev 3:10:** "Because you have kept my word of endurance, I will keep you from the hour of trial that is coming on the whole world to test all who live on the earth."
  Luke 8:15: "But that in the good soil is those who with a noble and good heart hear the word and hold it fast and bring forth fruit with endurance."

- **Rev 3:11a:** "I am coming in a short time."
  Luke 21:31b: "The kingdom of God is coming in a short time."

- **Rev 3:20:** "Look, I stand at the door and knock. If anyone hears my voice and opens the door, I will come in to him and eat with him, and he with me."
  Luke 12:36: "You are to be like people who are waiting for their lord to come home from the marriage feast, so that they may open to him at once when he comes and knocks."
  John 14:23: "If someone loves me, he will keep my word, and my Father will love him; and we will come to him and dwell with him."

This does not mean that they derive from the Gospels, however; rather, they stem from the wider environment of Christians who put words into Jesus' mouth to find answers for their uncertainties and problems. Another point should be stressed: although convinced that Jesus had dictated these texts, John clearly edited them. In the text below, the variations in font point to an advanced degree of stylization on John's part.

Strictly speaking, each letter is directed not to a church, but to the "angel of the community" who protected the church. This tutelary being lives in heaven and transmits the letter to the community. For an instructive analogy, see the notion of angels of various nations (Persia, Greece) found in Dan 10:13, 20.

The apostle Paul furnishes parallels for the way in which the prophet John received words of Jesus. When Paul was "in the third heaven" (2 Cor 12:2) and asked the risen Jesus to free him of a chronic infirmity (2 Cor 12:7–8), the reported answer was, "My grace is sufficient for you, for my power is made perfect in weakness" (2 Cor 12:9). This logion has not even a remote parallel in the Gospels. On another occasion, when Paul found it necessary to persuade the Thessalonian church that some would indeed survive to witness Jesus' return from heaven, he claimed it as a revelation that the Lord would descend from heaven in the near future. After that the dead would rise first and will be caught up together with the surviving Christians, including Paul, to meet the Lord in the air (1 Thess 4:15–17) and to be with him forever. This saying has echoes in Matt 24:30–31, 34 and again sheds light on how inauthentic sayings of Jesus came into existence and were passed on to others.

It must be remembered that upon entering the world of the Early Church one enters the world of fiction, fantasy, and sometimes even fraud (see 2 Thess 2:2). The first Christians and their successors tailored Jesus and his words to suit their present needs. The letters of John to the seven churches are filled with striking examples of this phenomenon.

The Letters to the Seven Churches

Revelation 2:1–7

Ephesus

¹To the angel of the church in Ephesus, write:

The words of him who holds the SEVEN stars in his *right hand*, who walks in the midst of the SEVEN GOLD *lampstands.*

²**I KNOW YOUR** WORKS, your toil, and your **endurance**, and (know) that you cannot *bear* evil people. And you have tested those who call themselves apostles but are not, and found them to be lying. ³And you have **endurance** and *have borne* on behalf of my name, and you have not become weary.

⁴But I have this against you: that you have abandoned your first love. ⁵Remember then from what you have fallen, REPENT, and do the WORKS you did at first. If not, I will come to you and remove your *lampstand* from its place, unless you REPENT.

⁶But you have this in your favor: you hate the works of the NICOLAITES, which I also hate.

⁷WHOEVER HAS AN EAR OUGHT TO HEAR WHAT THE SPIRIT SAYS TO THE CHURCHES.

TO THE VICTOR I will grant to eat of the tree of life, which is in the paradise of GOD.

Revelation 2:8–11
Smyrna

⁸And to the angel of the church in Smyrna, write:

The words of the first and the last, who died and came to life:

⁹**I KNOW YOUR** *tribulation* and poverty—but you are rich—and (I know) the slander of those WHO SAY THAT THEY ARE JEWS AND ARE NOT, but are a synagogue of SATAN.

¹⁰Do not fear what you will suffer. Look, the devil will throw some of you into prison, that you may be tested, and for ten days you will have *tribulation*. Be **FAITHFUL** unto death, and I will give you the crown of life.

¹¹WHOEVER HAS AN EAR OUGHT TO HEAR WHAT THE SPIRIT SAYS TO THE CHURCHES.

THE VICTOR shall not be hurt by the second death.

Revelation 2:12–17
Pergamum

¹²And to the angel of the church in Pergamum write:

The words of him who has the sharp and double-edged *SWORD*:

¹³I know where you *live*, where SATAN's throne is; yet you hold fast to my name and did not deny my **FAITH** even in the days of Antipas, my witness, my **FAITHFUL** one, who was killed among you, where SATAN *lives*.

¹⁴But I have a few things against you. *You have some* there *who hold the teaching* of Balaam, who taught Balak to entice the sons of Israel to sin that they might eat food sacrificed to idols and engage in fornication [cf. Num 31:16]. ¹⁵So *you* also *have some who hold the teaching of* the **NICOLAITES**.

[16]*REPENT*, then. If not, I will come to you quickly and war against them with the *SWORD* of my mouth.

[17]WHOEVER HAS AN EAR OUGHT TO HEAR WHAT THE SPIRIT SAYS TO THE CHURCHES.

TO THE VICTOR I shall give some of the hidden manna, and I will give him a white stone, and on the stone is written a new name that no one knows except the one who receives (it).

Revelation 2:18–29

Thyatira

[18]And to the angel of the church in Thyatira, write:

The words of the Son of God, who has eyes like a flame of fire, and whose feet are like burnished bronze:

[19]**I KNOW YOUR** WORKS, your love and *FAITH* and service and **endurance**, and that your latter WORKS exceed the first.

[20]But I have this against you, that you tolerate the woman Jezebel, who calls herself a prophetess and is *TEACHING* and be-guiling my servants to *fornicate* and to eat meat sacrificed to idols. [21]I have given her time to *REPENT*, but she refuses to *RE-PENT* of her *fornication*. [22]Look, I will throw her on a sickbed and those who commit adultery with her (I will throw) into great *tribulation* unless they *REPENT* of her WORKS. [23]And I will strike her children dead. And all the churches shall know that I am he who searches minds [lit. kidneys] and hearts and that I will give each of you in accordance with your WORKS.

[24]But to the rest of you in Thyatira, who do not hold this *TEACHING*, who do not know what some call the depths of Satan, to you I say that I do not lay on you any other burden; [25]only hold fast what you have, until I come.

[26]TO THE VICTOR, who keeps to my WORKS until the end, I will give authority over the nations, [27]and

> he shall rule them with a rod of iron,
> as when earthen pots are broken in pieces [Ps 2:9],

[28]even as I myself have received authority from my Father. And I will give him the morning star.

²⁹WHOEVER HAS AN EAR OUGHT TO HEAR WHAT THE SPIRIT
SAYS TO THE CHURCHES.

Revelation 3:1–6
Sardis

¹And to the angel of the church in Sardis write:

The words of him who has the seven spirits of GOD and the
seven stars:

I KNOW YOUR WORKS. You have the reputation of being
alive, but you are dead.

² *WATCH OUT*, and strengthen what remains and was on the
point of death, for I have not found your WORKS perfect in the
sight of my GOD. ³Remember then what you received and heard;
keep that, and *REPENT*. If you do not *WATCH OUT*, I will come like
a thief, and you will never know at what hour I will come upon
you.

⁴Yet you have still a few individuals in Sardis who have not
soiled their garments; and they shall walk with me in white, for
they are worthy.

⁵**THE VICTOR** shall thus be clothed in white garments,

I will not blot his *name* out of the book of life;
I will acknowledge his *name* before my Father and before
his angels.

⁶WHOEVER HAS AN EAR OUGHT TO HEAR WHAT THE SPIRIT SAYS
TO THE CHURCHES.

Revelation 3:7–13
Philadelphia

⁷To the angel of the church in Philadelphia, write:

The words of
the holy one,
the true one,
the one who has the key of David,
the one who opens and no one can shut,
the one who shuts and no one can open:

[8]**I KNOW YOUR** WORKS. Look, I have set before you an open door that no one is able to shut. You have (but) little strength, and yet you have kept my word and have not denied my name.

[9]Look, I will make those of the synagogue of Satan WHO SAY THAT THEY ARE JEWS AND ARE NOT, but are lying—look I will make them come and bow down before your feet, and learn that I have come love you.

[10]Because you have kept my word of endurance, I will keep you from the hour of trial that is coming on the whole world to test all who live on the earth.

[11]I am coming in a short time. Hold fast what you have, so that no one may seize your crown.

[12]**THE VICTOR** I will make into a pillar in the temple OF MY GOD, and he shall never go out of it. On him I will inscribe the *NAME* OF MY GOD and the *NAME* of the city OF MY GOD, the new Jerusalem, which comes down out of heaven from MY GOD, as well as my new *NAME*.

[13]WHOEVER HAS AN EAR OUGHT TO HEAR WHAT THE SPIRIT SAYS TO THE CHURCHES.

Revelation 3:14–21

Laodicea

[14]To the angel of the church in Laodicea, write:

The words of the Amen[1], the *FAITHFUL* and true witness, the beginning of GOD's creation:

[15]**I KNOW YOUR** WORKS. You are neither cold nor hot. Would that you were cold or hot. [16]So, because you are lukewarm, neither hot nor cold, I will spit you out of my mouth. [17]For you say, "I am *rich*, I have prospered, and I need nothing," not knowing that you are wretched, pitiable, poor, blind, and NAKED, [18]I counsel you

> to buy from me gold refined by fire
> so that you may be *rich*,
> and white garments

---

1. Description of God, cf. Isa 65:18.

so that you may clothe you
and the shame of your *NAKEDNESS* may not be seen,
and salve to anoint your eyes
so that you may see.

[19]Those whom I love, I reprove and chastise [cf. Prov 3:12].
Be zealous, then, and *REPENT.*

[20]Look, I stand at the door and knock. If anyone hears my voice and opens the door, I will come in to him and eat with him, and he with me.

[21]**TO THE VICTOR** I shall give the right to sit with me on my throne, as I myself first was **VICTORIOUS** and sit with my Father on his throne.

[22]WHOEVER HAS AN EAR OUGHT TO HEAR WHAT THE SPIRIT SAYS TO THE CHURCHES.

Index of New Testament Passages

131

Gerd Lüdemann is Professor of the History and Literature of Early Christianity, Director of the Institute of Early Christian Studies, and Founder and Director of the Archive "Religionsgeschichtliche Schule" at the University of Göttingen, Germany. He is also a Visiting Scholar at Vanderbilt Divinity School in Nashville, Tennessee, a Fellow of the Jesus Seminar, and has served as co-chair of the Society of Biblical Literature Seminar on Jewish Christianity. He is the author of many books including, *The Unholy in Holy Scripture* (1997), *The Great Deception* (1999), *Paul: The Founder of Christianity* (2002), *The Resurrection of Christ* (2004), *The Acts of the Apostles* (2005), *Intolerance and the Gospel* (2007), and *Eyes That See Not: The Pope Looks at Jesus* (2008).

CPSIA information can be obtained at www.ICGtesting.com
Printed in the USA
BVOW040438190112

280819BV00007B/38/P